WhatsApp's Culture Shift

WhatsApp's Culture Shift

Social Influence Explored

Sam Loray

UNIEK ENTERPRISES

CONTENTS

INDEX

Introduction

The coming of the computerized age has catalyzed a significant change in the manner people impart, separating boundaries and rising above topographical imperatives. Among the heap stages that have arisen as channels for this transformation, WhatsApp stands apart as a universal power, reshaping relational associations and social elements on a worldwide scale. In the previous ten years, the stage has gone through a wonderful development, progressing from a straightforward informing application to a diverse social environment. This transformation has changed the scene of individual correspondence as well as achieved a particular social shift — a peculiarity that warrants fastidious investigation.

WhatsApp, established in 2009 by Brian Acton and Jan Koum, started as an unassuming option in contrast to regular SMS informing. Its underlying allure lay in its effortlessness and cost-viability, giving clients a productive method for sending instant messages over the web. Notwithstanding, its genuine starting points misrepresented the seismic effect it would have on the social texture in the years to come. As the application built up momentum, it turned into a course for instant messages as well as for interactive media content, voice messages, and, in the end, video calls. The joining of these elements slowly changed WhatsApp from a utilitarian instrument into an extensive correspondence stage, working with a different cluster of communications.

The outcome of WhatsApp was powered by its practical abilities as well as by its obligation to client protection. Utilizing start to finish encryption, the stage guaranteed a solid climate for discussions, encouraging a feeling of trust among its clients. This obligation to security, combined with its easy to understand interface, added to the application's remarkable development, with billions of clients overall depending on it as their essential method for computerized correspondence.

The social ramifications of this shift are multi-layered and significant. WhatsApp has turned into an indispensable piece of day to day existence for the overwhelming majority, adjusting the elements of relational connections and cultural communications. The stage's impact stretches out past the domain of correspondence; it has saturated social standards, molding the manner in which individuals articulate their

"

thoughts, share data, and structure associations. This social effect is especially obvious with regards to social impact — a peculiarity that has taken on new aspects in the computerized age.

Social impact, an idea profoundly imbued in human collaborations, alludes to the manners by which people influence the contemplations, sentiments, and ways of behaving of others. In the advanced period, where virtual spaces reflect and, at times, rise above actual ones, social impact has tracked down new roads for articulation. WhatsApp, with its immense client base and various functionalities, has turned into a microcosm of these developing elements, offering experiences into the complicated interaction of impact, character, and correspondence.

One feature of WhatsApp's social effect lies in its job as a disseminator of data. The stage fills in as a conductor for the quick trade of information, feelings, and thoughts, frequently molding public talk and impacting aggregate discernments. The fast scattering of data, worked with by the application's ongoing nature, has significant ramifications for the arrangement of general assessment and the development of cultural stories. As messages overflow through interconnected networks, WhatsApp turns into an impetus for the intensification or constriction of specific points of view, adding to the molding of social standards.

In any case, the impact of WhatsApp goes past the simple transmission of data; it stretches out to the actual texture of relational connections. The stage's gathering talk highlight, specifically, has re-imagined the elements of groups of friends, making virtual spaces where people unite to share encounters, assessments, and feelings. These computerized networks, frequently crossing geological distances, act as pots for the development of shared characters and the support of social bonds. In this specific situation, WhatsApp goes about as a facilitator of social impact, permitting people to shape and be formed by the aggregate ethos of their picked computerized networks.

However, the social effect of WhatsApp isn't bound to the unequivocal trade of messages and data. The stage's connection point and highlights unpretentiously impact the idea of correspondence, forming the subtleties of articulation and collaboration. The presentation of emoticons, for example, has added a layer of profound profundity to message based discussions, rising above phonetic hindrances and working with nuanced types of articulation. Essentially, the status include, where clients can impart updates to their contacts, has turned into a material for self-articulation, adding to the development of computerized personas.

Also, the appearance of voice messages and video approaches WhatsApp has reclassified the surface of virtual communications. The capacity to convey tone, pitch, and looks progressively has brought a degree of promptness and realness to computerized discussions, overcoming any barrier among physical and virtual correspondence. Along these lines, WhatsApp's highlights act as utilitarian devices as well as instruments that shape the actual idea of human articulation and association in the advanced domain.

As WhatsApp keeps on developing, so too does its social effect. The stage's obtaining by Facebook in 2014 denoted a significant second in its direction, presenting new elements and reconciliations that further extended its compass and impact. The presentation of WhatsApp Business, for instance, changed the stage into a space for business cooperations, obscuring the lines among individual and expert correspondence. This convergence of business and individual life on a solitary stage has critical ramifications for the manners by which people explore and arrange their social universes.

The social shift actuated by WhatsApp is likewise clear in the domain of social activism. The stage has arisen as an amazing asset for coordinating, preparing, and scattering data on the side of different causes. From grassroots developments to huge scope fights, WhatsApp has worked with the fast spread of messages, empowering activists to arrange endeavors and intensify their effect. The decentralization of data stream on the stage difficulties conventional ordered progressions, engaging people to add to and shape stories on a worldwide scale.

In any case, the unavoidable impact of WhatsApp isn't without its difficulties. The stage has confronted examination for its job in the spread of deception and the enhancement of carefully protected areas. The start to finish encryption that guarantees client security likewise presents a difficulty with regards to tending to the abuse of the stage for odious purposes. Finding some kind of harmony between protecting security and relieving the hurtful impacts of deception represents a mind boggling challenge — one that requires consistent reconsideration of the stage's strategies and functionalities.

1. **Overview of WhatsApp's inception and growth**

   WhatsApp, brought into the world in the fruitful grounds of mechanical advancement, follows its foundations to the cooperative endeavors of Brian Acton and Jan Koum. It was 2009, and the team tried to address an essential correspondence challenge: the extravagant expenses related with sending instant messages through customary SMS. This beginning vision emerged into the making of WhatsApp, a basic yet progressive informing application that utilized the prospering force of the web to empower clients to send messages without causing SMS charges.

   The application's underlying allure lay in its usefulness and cost-adequacy. Clients could send instant messages, photographs, and recordings over the web, keeping away from the monetary requirements forced by customary transporters. The consistent client experience, combined with a pledge to protection through start to finish encryption, slung WhatsApp into the spotlight. Its development direction was out and out transient, drawing in clients universally who were looking for a dependable and secure option in contrast to customary informing stages.

   As WhatsApp got some decent forward momentum, it developed past its underlying job as a utilitarian informing application. The organizers' obligation to straightforwardness and client driven plan prepared for the continuous mix of extra highlights. Voice messages, bunch talks, and the capacity to share sight and sound substance extended the application's capacities, changing it into a complete correspondence stage. This transformation denoted the start of WhatsApp's excursion from a simple informing application to a diverse social environment.

The defining moment for WhatsApp came in 2014 when it was obtained by Facebook in a milestone bargain worth $19 billion. This procurement not just flagged the stage's entrance into the domain of web-based entertainment monsters yet in addition set up for its proceeded with extension and coordination with the more extensive Facebook environment.

The imbuement of assets and mastery from Facebook sped up WhatsApp's turn of events, introducing another time of development and advancement.

One of the key advancements post-securing was the acquaintance of end-with end encryption across all messages. This security highlight, intended to defend client protection, turned into a foundation of WhatsApp's character. It reverberated with clients who looked for a protected climate for their computerized discussions, setting WhatsApp's situation as a confided in stage for correspondence.

The client base of WhatsApp soar, arriving at billions worldwide. Its far and wide reception was not restricted to a specific segment or geological district; all things considered, it rose above social and etymological limits. The application turned into an essential piece of day to day existence for people, organizations, and networks, working with consistent correspondence and association on a worldwide scale.

The gathering visit include arose as a strong impetus for the stage's social elements. Empowering clients to make computerized networks, it encouraged a feeling of having a place and kinship. Companions, relatives, partners, and vested parties tracked down a virtual space inside WhatsApp to share encounters, conclusions, and updates. These advanced get-togethers became microcosms of true groups of friends, affecting the manners by which people shaped and kept up with connections.

Past private correspondence, WhatsApp's impact ventured into the domains of business and trade with the presentation of WhatsApp Business. This expansion of the stage took care of the requirements of endeavors, permitting them to interface with clients, share refreshes, and work with exchanges. The incorporation of business functionalities into the application obscured the lines among individual and expert correspondence, mirroring the advancing idea of computerized connections.

The social effect of WhatsApp is complicatedly woven into the texture of how individuals articulate their thoughts in the computerized age. Emoticons, when an eccentric expansion to message based discussions, turned into a widespread language of feeling, rising above phonetic hindrances. The status highlight, where clients share brief updates with their contacts, turned into a material for self-articulation and character development. The presentation of voice messages and video calls added layers of closeness to computerized discussions, overcoming any barrier among virtual and actual association.

WhatsApp's social reverberation isn't bound to the unequivocal trade of messages. It stretches out to the certain standards and ways of behaving that describe computerized correspondence. The stage, with its ongoing nature and steady availability, has reshaped the beat and mood of relational collaborations.

The instantaneousness of reactions, the nonconcurrent idea of discussions, and the nonstop progression of data add to a remarkable computerized rhythm that recognizes WhatsApp from other correspondence channels.

In the circle of data spread, WhatsApp arose as a strong power, impacting popular assessment and molding stories. The stage turned into a course for the quick trade of information, suppositions, and thoughts. Be that as it may, this recently discovered power was not without challenges. WhatsApp confronted examination for its job in the spread of falsehood, counterfeit news, and the making of carefully protected areas. The decentralized idea of data stream on the stage presented complex predicaments, requiring a fragile harmony between protecting client security and moderating the unsafe impacts of deception.

WhatsApp's social effect reaches out past individual communications to envelop more extensive social peculiarities, including social activism. The stage turned into a preparation instrument for activists and backing gatherings, giving a decentralized space to coordinating and dispersing data. From grassroots developments to enormous scope fights, WhatsApp assumed a part in enhancing the voices of those pushing for social and political change.

As WhatsApp keeps on advancing, its social impact continues and adjusts to the consistently changing scene of the computerized age. The stage's development from a straightforward informing application to a worldwide social environment mirrors the unique interchange between mechanical advancement, client conduct, and social elements. The investigation of WhatsApp's origin and development fills in as an essential comprehension of the stage's social importance, making way for a more profound assessment of its multi-layered influence on society, correspondence, and human association.

2. **Significance of WhatsApp in the realm of digital communication**

In the immense and dynamic scene of computerized correspondence, WhatsApp remains as a transcending presence, using critical impact over how people associate, share, and connect in the 21st 100 years. Its direction from an unassuming informing application to a worldwide social environment has denoted a change in perspective in the manner individuals impart, rising above geological limits and reshaping social standards. The meaning of WhatsApp in the domain of computerized correspondence is multi-layered, enveloping mechanical advancement, social elements, and the development of human association.

At its center, WhatsApp addresses an innovative wonder that use the force of the web to work with ongoing correspondence. The application's initiation tended to a squeezing need: the expense and limits related with customary SMS informing. By empowering clients to send instant messages, photographs, recordings, and voice messages over the web, WhatsApp democratized correspondence, freeing it from the requirements of costly transporter based administrations.

This mechanical development assumed an essential part in extending admittance to specialized apparatuses, especially in districts where customary informing administrations were monetarily difficult.

The obligation to client protection through start to finish encryption further recognizes WhatsApp in the domain of computerized correspondence. In a period where worries about information security and protection are fundamental, WhatsApp's execution of vigorous encryption conventions has situated it as a confided in stage for delicate discussions. This responsibility resounds with clients who focus on secure correspondence, encouraging a feeling of trust that has added to the stage's boundless reception.

The development of WhatsApp from an informing application to a complete correspondence stage addresses a consistent joining of elements that take care of different client needs. Voice messages, bunch visits, video calls, and media sharing capacities have changed the application into a flexible device that obliges a range of correspondence styles. This flexibility is a vital consider WhatsApp's supported significance, as it keeps on gathering the developing inclinations and assumptions for its different client base.

The meaning of WhatsApp reaches out past its utilitarian functionalities to envelop its job in forming social elements. The stage has turned into a virtual space where people, networks, and organizations meet to interface and convey. The gathering talk highlight, specifically, has reclassified the elements of groups of friends, giving a computerized climate where clients share encounters, feelings, and updates progressively. These computerized networks, frequently rising above topographical limits, act as center points for the development of connections and the trading of thoughts.

With regards to individual connections, WhatsApp has turned into a fundamental piece of day to day existence. Loved ones use the stage to remain associated, share minutes, and direction exercises. The instantaneousness of correspondence worked with by WhatsApp has compacted the worldly and spatial components of relational collaborations, permitting people to keep a steady and constant association regardless of actual distance. The stage has, generally, become a computerized help for individual connections, molding the musicality and rhythm of current correspondence.

Past special interactions, WhatsApp has saturated the expert circle with the presentation of WhatsApp Business. This expansion of the stage takes care of the requirements of organizations, empowering them to speak with clients, share refreshes, and work with exchanges. The combination of business functionalities into WhatsApp obscures the lines among individual and expert correspondence, mirroring the liquid idea of advanced connections in contemporary society. Subsequently, the stage has turned into a course for both individual and business trades, further cementing its status as a complete correspondence biological system.

The social meaning of WhatsApp is substantial in the manner it has impacted the actual surface of human articulation in the computerized age. Emoticons, when considered energetic increases to message based discussions, have turned into a widespread language of feeling, rising above semantic and social hindrances. The status highlight, where clients share brief updates or mixed media satisfied with their contacts, has turned into a material for self-articulation, permitting people to art and curate their computerized personas.

The presentation of voice messages and video approaches WhatsApp has added layers of closeness to computerized discussions. The capacity to convey tone, pitch, and looks continuously overcomes any barrier among virtual and actual association, enhancing the informative experience. Along these lines, WhatsApp not just fills in as a useful device for correspondence yet in addition as a medium that shapes the subtleties of human articulation and association in the computerized domain.

The stage's social effect is additionally highlighted by its job as a disseminator of data. The fast trade of information, feelings, and thoughts on WhatsApp has significant ramifications for the arrangement of general assessment and the development of cultural stories. As messages overflow through interconnected networks, WhatsApp turns into an impetus for the intensification or weakening of specific points of view, adding to the molding of social standards.

In any case, the meaning of WhatsApp in data spread isn't without its difficulties. The stage has confronted analysis for its part in the spread of falsehood and the making of carefully protected areas. The decentralized idea of data stream on WhatsApp, while safeguarding client protection, presents complex issues in tending to the destructive impacts of falsehood. Finding some kind of harmony between safeguarding protection and alleviating the likely abuse of the stage stays a continuous test, highlighting the requirement for constant assessment and transformation of strategies and functionalities.

In the domain of social impact, WhatsApp has arisen as a microcosm of developing elements. The gathering talk highlight, specifically, works with the arrangement of advanced networks where people meet around shared interests, encounters, or affiliations. These people group become cauldrons for the development of shared personalities and the support of social bonds. Inside these computerized spaces, people get data as well as effectively add to the development of aggregate accounts, impacting and being affected by the ethos of their picked networks.

The stage's impact stretches out past special interactions to the more extensive circle of social activism. WhatsApp has turned into an incredible asset for coordinating, preparing, and spreading data on the side of different causes. From grassroots developments to enormous scope dissents, the stage works with the fast spread of messages, empowering activists to organize endeavors and intensify their effect. This decentralization of data stream difficulties customary orders, enabling people to add to and shape stories on a worldwide scale.

The obtaining of WhatsApp by Facebook in 2014 denoted a significant second in its direction. The implantation of assets and aptitude from Facebook sped up the stage's turn of events, introducing new elements and mixes. The cooperative connection among WhatsApp and Facebook broadened the compass of the two stages, making collaborations that further set WhatsApp's situation in the advanced correspondence scene.

Nonetheless, the inescapable impact of WhatsApp isn't without its doubters. The stage has been condemned for its capability to add to social detachment, as steady network through informing applications can prompt a feeling of computerized overpower and the disintegration of eye to eye cooperations. Moreover, worries about the habit-forming nature of steady notices and the effect on emotional wellness have been raised, provoking a more extensive cultural discussion about the harmony between computerized network and prosperity.

All in all, the meaning of WhatsApp in the domain of advanced correspondence is significant and extensive. From its beginning as an informing application addressing the expense requirements of conventional SMS to its ongoing status as a worldwide social environment, WhatsApp plays had a groundbreaking impact in forming how people associate, convey, and impact each other in the computerized age. Its mechanical development, obligation to client security, and versatility to advancing client needs have added to its broad reception and social reverberation. As WhatsApp proceeds to develop and adjust, its importance as a social power and an impetus for cultural change will without a doubt persevere, highlighting its getting through influence on the texture of human association in the 21st 100 years.

3. **Thesis statement: Exploring the cultural shift and social influence brought about by WhatsApp**

At the crossing point of innovation and human collaboration, WhatsApp arises as an extraordinary power that has induced a social shift and employed critical social impact. The stage, brought into the world in 2009 as a straightforward informing application, has developed into a worldwide social biological system, reshaping the elements of relational connections, data spread, and cultural stories. This investigation dives into the complex components of WhatsApp's social effect, navigating its origin, development, mechanical advancements, and the many-sided exchange between friendly elements and computerized correspondence.

WhatsApp's process starts with its pioneers, Brian Acton and Jan Koum, trying to address the monetary limitations related with customary SMS informing. The application's progressive methodology, permitting clients to send messages over the web without causing SMS charges, established the groundwork for a change in outlook in computerized correspondence. From its unassuming starting points, WhatsApp quickly acquired ubiquity, driven by its obligation to client protection through start to finish encryption and an easy to understand interface.

The stage's importance lies in its mechanical advancement as well as in its versatility to developing client needs. WhatsApp changed from a utilitarian informing application into an exhaustive correspondence stage, offering elements, for example, voice messages, bunch talks, video calls, and sight and sound sharing. This extension not just expanded the utilitarian abilities of the application yet in addition extended its social effect, situating it as a fundamental piece of day to day existence for billions of clients around the world.

A significant second in WhatsApp's direction happened in 2014 when Facebook gained the stage in a noteworthy $19 billion arrangement. This securing denoted the mixture of assets and skill starting with one tech goliath then onto the next, catalyzing further development and combination. WhatsApp's digestion into the Facebook environment set up for new highlights, extended functionalities, and an expanded client base, hardening its status as a worldwide correspondence force to be reckoned with.

Protection, a foundation of WhatsApp's character, has been a main thrust behind its broad reception. The execution of start to finish encryption guarantees secure correspondence, encouraging a feeling of trust among clients. This obligation to protection, combined with the stage's consistent client experience, plays had a significant impact in molding WhatsApp's social impact and settling on it a favored decision for computerized correspondence.

The social shift actuated by WhatsApp appears in different aspects of human connection, starting with the stage's job in private connections. The promptness and continuous nature of WhatsApp have compacted worldly and spatial limits, empowering people to keep up with steady and personal associations regardless of actual distances. The stage has turned into a computerized help for loved ones, modifying the beat and rhythm of current correspondence.

Fundamental to WhatsApp's social effect is the gathering talk include, which encourages the arrangement of computerized networks. These people group, frequently rising above geological limits, act as centers for the development of shared personalities and the support of social bonds. Inside these virtual spaces, people effectively add to the development of aggregate stories, impacting and being affected by the ethos of their picked networks. The gathering visit highlight changes WhatsApp from a simple specialized device into a powerful field for social collaboration and impact.

WhatsApp's impact reaches out past unique interactions into the expert circle with the presentation of WhatsApp Business. This augmentation of the stage takes care of the requirements of organizations, working with correspondence with clients, sharing updates, and empowering exchanges. The combination of business functionalities into WhatsApp obscures the lines among individual and expert correspondence, mirroring the liquid idea of advanced cooperations in contemporary society.

The social meaning of WhatsApp is additionally highlighted by its effect on human articulation in the advanced age. Emoticons, when considered lively increments to message based discussions, have developed into a widespread language of feeling, rising above phonetic and social obstructions. The status include, where clients share brief updates or sight and sound substance, fills in as a material for self-articulation, permitting people to specialty and curate their computerized personas.

The presentation of voice messages and video approaches WhatsApp adds layers of closeness to advanced discussions. Continuous correspondence, complete with tone, pitch, and looks, overcomes any issues among virtual and actual collaboration, advancing the open insight. WhatsApp works with useful correspondence as well as shapes the actual subtleties of how people articulate their thoughts and interface with others in the computerized domain.

WhatsApp's importance in data scattering is crucial, impacting popular assessment and cultural stories. The stage fills in as a course for the fast trade of information, conclusions, and thoughts, molding the development of social standards. Be that as it may, this impact isn't without challenges, as WhatsApp has confronted examination for its part in the spread of falsehood and the making of protected, closed off environments. The decentralized idea of data stream on the stage, while protecting client security, presents complex predicaments in tending to the expected abuse for loathsome purposes.

In the domain of social activism, WhatsApp has arisen as an integral asset for coordinating, preparing, and dispersing data on the side of different causes. From grassroots developments to enormous scope dissents, the stage works with the quick spread of messages, empowering activists to organize endeavors and intensify their effect. This decentralization of data stream difficulties customary pecking orders, engaging people to add to and shape stories on a worldwide scale.

The procurement of WhatsApp by Facebook denoted a urgent second in its direction. The advantageous connection between the two stages expanded their span, making cooperative energies that further cemented WhatsApp's situation in the computerized correspondence scene. Be that as it may, the stage's inescapable impact isn't without analysis. Worries about friendly detachment, the habit-forming nature of consistent warnings, and the effect on psychological well-being have provoked a more extensive cultural discussion about the harmony between computerized network and prosperity.

As WhatsApp proceeds to develop and adjust to the steadily changing scene of the advanced age, its social importance perseveres. The stage's development from a basic informing application to a worldwide social biological system mirrors the unique interaction between mechanical development, client conduct, and social elements.

WhatsApp's investigation stretches out past its utilitarian viewpoints to envelop a more profound comprehension of its job as a social power, impacting the texture of human association and cultural elements in the 21st 100 years.

Chapter 1

The Evolution of Digital Communication

The development of computerized correspondence has been a groundbreaking excursion that has fundamentally influenced the way people, organizations, and social orders connect. From the beginning of essential electronic correspondence to the refined and interconnected organizations of the present, the advancement has been fast and diverse.

The groundwork of advanced correspondence can be followed back to the development of the message in the nineteenth 100 years. Samuel Morse's improvement of Morse code in 1837 denoted a huge jump forward in significant distance correspondence. The message permitted messages to be sent over huge spans utilizing electrical signs, laying the foundation for future progressions in electronic correspondence.

As the twentieth century unfolded, the phone arose as a progressive development, empowering ongoing voice correspondence between people isolated by immense distances. The expansion of phone lines and the foundation of a worldwide media communications framework denoted a significant jump in the development of correspondence. The capacity to talk straightforwardly to somebody, paying little heed to geological obstructions, was a historic improvement that laid the preparation for the computerized age.

The mid-twentieth century saw the approach of PCs, which would assume a critical part in molding the eventual fate of computerized correspondence. At first, PCs were enormous, costly machines utilized principally for logical and military purposes. Be that as it may, with headways in innovation, PCs turned out to be more available to the overall population. The improvement of the ARPANET in the last part of the 1960s, the forerunner to the cutting edge web, denoted a urgent defining moment in the development of computerized correspondence.

The 1970s and 1980s saw the introduction of email, a specialized instrument that would reform the manner in which individuals traded data. Email gave a quicker and more productive option in contrast to customary mail, permitting clients to electronically send messages. This advancement laid the foundation for the improvement of computerized informing stages and set up for the interconnected world we live in today.

The 1990s saw the ascent of the Internet, a decentralized arrangement of data trade that changed the web into an easy to use and open stage. The presentation of internet browsers made it feasible for people to explore the web easily, opening up additional opportunities for correspondence, data sharing, and joint effort. The idea of informal communication arose, making ready for stages that would reclassify the idea of relational correspondence.

With the new thousand years came the multiplication of cell phones and the approach of remote correspondence. Cell phones developed from straightforward voice specialized gadgets to strong, pocket-sized PCs fit for getting to the web, sending messages, and running a horde of uses. The accommodation of portable correspondence added to the rising interconnectedness of the worldwide populace.

The ascent of web-based entertainment stages in the 21st century further changed advanced correspondence. Stages like Facebook, Twitter, and Instagram became virtual spaces where people could share contemplations, encounters, and sight and sound substance with a worldwide crowd. The idea of long range interpersonal communication reached out past special interactions to envelop business, governmental issues, and activism, it is scattered and consumed to shape the way data.

As innovation kept on propelling, the advancement of fast web and broadband network became pivotal for working with consistent computerized correspondence. The change from dial-up to broadband denoted a huge improvement in information move speeds, empowering the web based of mixed media content, video conferencing, and other data transmission concentrated exercises.

The appearance of cell phones with high velocity portable information further sped up the development of computerized correspondence. Portable applications, or "applications," became necessary to the manner in which individuals impart, work, and engage themselves.

Informing applications, specifically, acquired unmistakable quality, offering elements, for example, texting, voice and video calls, and sight and sound sharing.

The development of video conferencing stages turned out to be especially huge with regards to remote work and virtual joint effort. The Coronavirus pandemic in the mid 2020s featured the significance of advanced specialized apparatuses in keeping up with business tasks and relational associations during seasons of physical removing.

Computerized reasoning (man-made intelligence) has additionally transformed advanced correspondence, with chatbots, remote helpers, and language handling calculations improving the client experience. These artificial intelligence controlled instruments have robotized routine assignments, worked with regular language associations, and customized correspondence, making advanced stages more natural and easy to understand.

The Web of Things (IoT) addresses one more wilderness in the development of advanced correspondence. The interconnectivity of gadgets, from brilliant home machines to modern sensors, has made a trap of correspondence that stretches out past human cooperation. This interconnected organization of gadgets can possibly alter different enterprises, from medical care to transportation, by empowering consistent correspondence between machines.

Blockchain innovation, at first created for cryptographic forms of money like Bitcoin, has additionally tracked down applications in advanced correspondence. The decentralized and secure nature of blockchain can possibly improve the protection and trustworthiness of correspondence, offering answers for issues, for example, information breaks and unapproved access.

The fate of advanced correspondence holds invigorating conceivable outcomes with the continuous improvement of innovations like 5G, increased reality (AR), and computer generated reality (VR). 5G organizations vow to convey quicker and more solid network, empowering imaginative applications, for example, expanded reality encounters and continuous correspondence with insignificant inertness.

Expanded reality overlays computerized data onto the actual world, making vivid encounters that mix the virtual and genuine. Augmented reality, then again, transports clients to altogether advanced conditions, offering new aspects for correspondence, joint effort, and diversion. These advancements can possibly rethink how people connect with computerized content and one another.

All in all, the development of computerized correspondence has been a dynamic and persistent cycle, formed by mechanical headways, cultural requirements, and human advancement. From the message to the web, from email to virtual entertainment, every achievement has united us, separating the boundaries of reality.

As we plan ahead, the continuous improvement of innovations, for example, 5G, artificial intelligence, IoT, and blockchain vows to additionally alter the manner in which we impart, opening up additional opportunities and difficulties not too far off of the computerized age.

1.1 Historical context of digital communication platforms

The verifiable setting of computerized correspondence stages is a story that unfurls across many years, complicatedly woven into the texture of mechanical progressions, cultural movements, and the persevering quest for interconnectedness. To comprehend the advancement of computerized correspondence stages, we should travel back to the early foundations of processing and the rise of innovations that made ready for the interconnected world we possess today.

The mid-twentieth century denoted a critical defining moment with the approach of PCs. At first huge, cumbersome machines principally used for logical and military purposes, PCs started to advance with regards to availability and usefulness. The 1950s and 1960s saw the improvement of early PC organizations, establishing the groundwork for the interconnected frameworks that would later turn into the foundation of computerized correspondence.

The introduction of the ARPANET in the last part of the 1960s stands apart as a critical second in the verifiable direction of computerized correspondence stages. Made by the U.S. Division of Safeguard's High level Exploration Tasks Organization (ARPA), the ARPANET was the forerunner to the cutting edge web. Its basic role was to lay out a decentralized and hearty correspondence network that could endure the likely obliteration of individual hubs, a worry established in Cool Conflict period nerves.

The ARPANET's improvement presented the idea of parcel exchanging, a strategy for partitioning information into bundles for more effective transmission across the organization. This leading edge development took into consideration the production of a decentralized correspondence foundation, shaping the reason for the web's versatility and flexibility. The ARPANET's fruitful transmission of the principal message between two far off PCs in 1969 denoted the start of another time in computerized correspondence.

The 1970s saw the refinement of email for of electronic correspondence. Beam Tomlinson, an ARPANET engineer, is credited with sending the primary email in 1971, utilizing the recognizable "user@host" design that continues today. Email immediately acquired ubiquity as a quicker and more productive option in contrast to conventional mail, changing the manner in which people and associations traded data.

The 1980s delivered the improvement of the Space Name Framework (DNS), an essential part of the web that deciphers comprehensible space names into IP addresses. This advancement worked on the most common way of exploring the developing web, making it more open to the overall population.

With the presentation of internet browsers like Mosaic in the mid 1990s, the Internet turned into an easy to understand interface, making ready for the mass reception of computerized correspondence stages.

The ascent of the web as a public utility during the 1990s harmonized with the development of early computerized correspondence stages. Web Transfer Visit (IRC) permitted constant text-based correspondence between clients, laying the basis for later talk stages. Notice Board Frameworks (BBS) gave online gatherings to conversations, record sharing, and informing, making virtual networks that foreshadowed the social idea of current advanced stages.

The last part of the 1990s and mid 2000s saw the multiplication of texting (IM) stages, further molding the scene of computerized correspondence. Administrations like ICQ, AOL Moment Courier (Point), and MSN Courier permitted clients to take part continuously text-based discussions, separating geological obstructions and empowering prompt correspondence. The prevalence of IM laid the preparation for the future advancement of more modern and component rich informing stages.

The beginning of the 21st century achieved the ascent of web-based entertainment stages, in a general sense changing the idea of computerized correspondence. Friendster, sent off in 2002, is in many cases credited as one of the principal person to person communication destinations, permitting clients to interface with companions and grow their groups of friends on the web. MySpace, Facebook, and LinkedIn before long followed, each taking care of various parts of social collaboration, individual articulation, and expert systems administration.

Facebook, established by Imprint Zuckerberg in 2004, arose as an extraordinary power in the domain of web-based entertainment. Its accentuation on genuine name character, client profiles, and the News channel laid the preparation for a more private and interconnected internet based insight. The stage's quick development and worldwide arrive at flagged a change in the manner individuals drew in with computerized correspondence, moving past the limits of informing and email to a more vivid and dynamic web-based presence.

Twitter, sent off in 2006, presented the idea of microblogging, permitting clients to share short messages, or tweets, with a worldwide crowd. The stage's continuous nature and effortlessness added to its broad reception as an instrument for sharing news, feelings, and updates. Twitter exemplified the developing scene of advanced correspondence stages, underlining promptness and quickness.

The ascent of cell phones in the last part of the 2000s further sped up the development of computerized correspondence. Versatile informing applications like WhatsApp, sent off in 2009, and later stages, for example, Snapchat and Instagram, profited by the omnipresence of cell phones to convey mixed media rich correspondence encounters.

These applications worked with text-based discussions as well as the sharing of photographs, recordings, and ongoing updates, reshaping the manner in which individuals imparted and communicated their thoughts on the web.

Video content turned out to be progressively common with the approach of stages like YouTube, which permitted clients to transfer, share, and find recordings on a worldwide scale. The ascent of live streaming stages, for example, Jerk and Periscope further stressed the interest for constant, intuitive substance. Computerized correspondence stages were not generally bound to static text or pictures; they had developed into dynamic spaces where clients could participate in live discussions and offer encounters continuously.

The idea of "long range informal communication" extended past special interactions to include proficient systems administration on stages like LinkedIn and cooperative systems administration on stages like GitHub. Online people group thrived, uniting people with shared interests, whether in gaming, programming, or specialty leisure activities. The broadening of advanced correspondence stages mirrored the complex idea of human connection and cooperation.

The reconciliation of voice and video calls into informing stages denoted one more huge development in advanced correspondence. Administrations like Skype, at first sent off in 2003, made ready for stages like FaceTime, Zoom, and Microsoft Groups, which acquired unmistakable quality during the 2010s. The Coronavirus pandemic in 2020 further highlighted the significance of video conferencing as a fundamental device for remote work, schooling, and social connection.

Man-made consciousness (simulated intelligence) assumed a filling part in molding computerized correspondence stages. Chatbots became omnipresent, giving robotized reactions and help with different web-based collaborations. Remote helpers like Siri, Alexa, and Google Right hand presented normal language handling and voice acknowledgment, upgrading the client experience and growing the manners by which people associated with innovation.

The approach of the Web of Things (IoT) acquainted another aspect with computerized correspondence, expanding network past conventional processing gadgets. Brilliant gadgets, going from indoor regulators to wearables, conveyed consistently with one another, making an environment of interconnected gadgets. This interconnectedness laid the basis for savvy homes, brilliant urban areas, and advancements in medical care, transportation, and different ventures.

Blockchain innovation, initially produced for digital forms of money, tracked down applications in getting computerized correspondence. The decentralized and alter safe nature of blockchain offered answers for issues like information security, protection, and validation.

Blockchain-based stages investigated the potential for decentralized online entertainment, empowering clients to have more prominent command over their information and collaborations.

Planning ahead, the continuous advancement of 5G innovation vows to reform computerized correspondence stages. With quicker information speeds, lower dormancy, and expanded network limit, 5G makes the way for additional opportunities like increased reality (AR) and augmented reality (VR) encounters. These vivid advances can possibly reclassify how people impart, work together, and experience computerized content.

All in all, the verifiable setting of computerized correspondence stages is a story of development, variation, and cultural change. From the beginning of PC organizations to the ascent of online entertainment and the incorporation of trend setting innovations like computer based intelligence and IoT, each stage mirrors the developing necessities and desires of an associated world. As we go on into the future, the convergence of arising advances and human creativity will without a doubt shape the following parts in the continuous development of computerized correspondence stages.

1.2 Emergence of messaging apps and their societal impact

The rise of informing applications has fundamentally changed the scene of computerized correspondence, reshaping the manner in which people associate, impart, and share data. The development of these stages reflects mechanical headways as well as significant changes in cultural ways of behaving, assumptions, and methods of communication.

The mid 2000s saw the ascent of texting (IM) as a famous type of online correspondence. Stages like AOL Moment Courier (Point), ICQ, and MSN Courier became fundamental pieces of the computerized insight, permitting clients to take part progressively text-based discussions. These stages denoted a takeoff from conventional email, offering an additional prompt and dynamic method for correspondence that resounded with clients looking for moment delight in their web-based collaborations.

As the fame of IM developed, so did the interest for more adaptable and highlight rich informing stages. The appearance of cell phones and versatile applications in the last part of the 2000s gave an impetus to the following stage in the development of computerized correspondence. Informing applications arose as independent applications, utilizing the capacities of cell phones to offer a consistent and intelligent correspondence experience.

WhatsApp, sent off in 2009, played a spearheading job in the mass reception of versatile informing applications. With its easy to use connection point and obligation to start to finish encryption, WhatsApp gave a safe and helpful stage for text informing, voice calls, and media sharing. The application's prosperity exhibited a change in client inclinations towards more private, moment, and mixed media rich correspondence.

The cultural effect of informing applications turned out to be progressively obvious as these stages advanced. One of the key changes was the obscuring of individual and expert correspondence. Informing applications worked with fast and casual correspondence, separating the hindrances among individual and work life. This shift had suggestions for working environment elements, presenting new methods of coordinated effort and correspondence that rose above customary office limits.

The worldwide idea of informing applications additionally added to the peculiarity of virtual connectedness. Companions, relatives, and partners could now convey continuously, paying little heed to geological distances. This reinforced existing connections as well as took into consideration the development of new associations, encouraging a feeling of a universally interconnected local area.

Social elements went through a change too, with the ascent of gathering informing highlights on stages like WhatsApp and Message. Bunch visits became spaces for aggregate direction, occasion arranging, and easygoing discussions. They became virtual centers where people could share contemplations, updates, and media with a select gathering of contacts, making miniature networks inside the bigger organization of computerized associations.

The incorporation of voice and video calls inside informing applications further extended the extent of advanced correspondence. Applications like Skype, FaceTime, and later, WhatsApp and Zoom, permitted clients to participate progressively sound and video discussions. This improved the close to home profundity of correspondence as well as addressed the requirement for eye to eye communications in an undeniably computerized world.

The impact of informing applications stretched out past private collaborations to cultural and political domains. These stages became conductors for data dispersal, activism, and social developments. During occasions, for example, the Middle Easterner Spring and Possess Money Road, informing applications assumed a vital part in sorting out fights, sharing ongoing updates, and planning aggregate activity. The quickness and reach of these stages turned out to be integral assets for grassroots developments looking to impact change.

Protection concerns arose as a huge cultural thought with the boundless utilization of informing applications. While the encryption highlights of stages like WhatsApp gave an elevated degree of safety for clients' correspondence, it additionally started banters about the harmony among protection and public safety. Legislatures, policing, and tech organizations wound up exploring an intricate scene where the right to protection conflicted with the requirement for reconnaissance and public security.

The convergence of informing applications with web-based entertainment stages additionally obscured the lines among private and public correspondence. The presentation of highlights like Stories on stages like Instagram and Snapchat permitted clients to impart fleeting substance to their organizations. This change in satisfied sharing brought up issues about the lastingness of computerized correspondence and its effect on individual and aggregate memory.

As informing applications became indispensable to day to day existence, their effect on language and correspondence standards became obvious. The utilization of emoticons, GIFs, and stickers became normal types of articulation, rising above etymological hindrances and adding a layer of subtlety to computerized discussions. Shortened forms, abbreviations, and web shoptalk tracked down their direction into regular correspondence, molding a computerized dictionary that mirrored the casual and high speed nature of informing.

Organizations additionally perceived the capability of informing applications as incredible assets for client commitment. Many organizations embraced chatbots on stages like Facebook Courier to give moment client service, answer inquiries, and work with exchanges. This undeniable a shift towards more customized and intelligent client cooperations, underscoring the significance of promptness and openness in the business-buyer relationship.

The instructive scene went through a change with the coordination of informing applications into learning conditions. Instructive foundations and educators utilized stages like WhatsApp and Slack to work with correspondence, share assets, and direct virtual classes. The instantaneousness of informing applications gave understudies direct admittance to teachers, cultivating a more powerful and intelligent growth opportunity.

The Coronavirus pandemic in 2020 sped up the cultural dependence on informing applications and computerized correspondence stages. With lockdowns and social removing estimates set up, individuals went to these apparatuses for work, schooling, and keeping up with social associations. Video conferencing stages became life savers for remote work and virtual social occasions, featuring the versatility and flexibility of computerized correspondence advancements in the midst of emergency.

While the effect of informing applications on society has been to a great extent certain, difficulties and concerns have likewise arisen. The spread of deception, cyberbullying, and the habit-forming nature of steady availability are issues that society wrestles with as these stages keep on advancing. Finding some kind of harmony between the advantages and downsides of computerized correspondence stays a consistent test for people, networks, and policymakers.

Looking forward, the eventual fate of informing applications holds the commitment of proceeded with advancement and incorporation with arising innovations. The improvement of chatbots, man-made brainpower, and expanded reality could additionally upgrade the capacities of these stages, offering clients more customized and vivid correspondence encounters.

As innovation keeps on propelling, society will without a doubt see new elements of effect and change in the manner people interface and convey in the computerized age.

1.3 WhatsApp's unique role in shaping modern communication dynamics

WhatsApp, established in 2009 by Brian Acton and Jan Koum, has assumed an extraordinary and groundbreaking part in molding present day correspondence elements. From its origin as a basic informing application to its ongoing status as a worldwide stage with more than two billion clients, WhatsApp has turned into a fundamental piece of how people, organizations, and networks convey and interface. Inspecting its advancement and effect gives significant bits of knowledge into the more extensive scene of computerized correspondence.

In its initial days, WhatsApp entered a serious market overwhelmed by texting stages like AOL Moment Courier, ICQ, and MSN Courier. What put WhatsApp aside was its obligation to straightforwardness, client security, and an emphasis on continuous correspondence. The application's originators planned to make an instrument that repeated the quickness and closeness of eye to eye discussions, a dream that would fundamentally impact the application's plan and usefulness.

One of WhatsApp's particular highlights was its commitment to start to finish encryption, presented in 2014. This safety effort guaranteed that main the planned beneficiary could unscramble and peruse the messages, giving a degree of protection and security that reverberated with clients. In a period when worries about information security were on the ascent, WhatsApp's solid encryption turned into a pivotal differentiator, separating it from other informing stages.

The application's outcome in focusing on client protection and security added to its fast worldwide reception. WhatsApp's client base extended past individual clients to incorporate organizations, associations, and even legislatures. Its cross-stage similarity and accessibility on the two iOS and Android gadgets further worked with inescapable use, making it open to a wide and various crowd.

WhatsApp's effect on present day correspondence elements is obvious in its job as a device for individual and expert connections. As an informing application, it gave a helpful and savvy option in contrast to customary SMS, particularly for global correspondence. The stage's utilization of web information for informing as opposed to conventional cell networks made it an appealing choice for clients looking to keep away from SMS charges.

The presentation of voice bringing in 2015 and video bringing in 2016 extended WhatsApp's capacities, changing it into a far reaching correspondence stage. Clients could now make great voice and video brings over Wi-Fi or versatile information, further lessening the dependence on conventional media communications framework. This development lined up with the more extensive pattern of computerized correspondence stages incorporating different methods of communication into a solitary connection point.

WhatsApp's job in associating networks and cultivating social cooperations turned out to be especially clear with the ascent of gathering informing. Bunch visits permitted clients to make virtual spaces for family, companions, partners, and interest-based networks, empowering continuous discussions and media dividing between a select gathering of people. This component reflected the social elements of disconnected networks, uniting individuals in a computerized space to share encounters, data, and updates.

The application's impact reached out past special interactions to proficient settings, testing the customary limits among individual and business related correspondence. Little and medium-sized organizations embraced WhatsApp as a device for client commitment, request handling, and offering ongoing help. Its availability and usability made it an optimal stage for organizations to associate with clients, fabricate connections, and smooth out correspondence processes.

WhatsApp Business, a committed rendition of the application for private companies, further worked with this pattern. Sent off in 2018, WhatsApp Business offered highlights like business profiles, robotized informing, and the capacity to connection to a business' site. These highlights enabled organizations to lay out a computerized presence, discuss straightforwardly with clients, and improve the general client experience.

WhatsApp's effect on cultural and political elements turned out to be especially articulated in districts where the application accomplished far reaching reception. In certain nations, WhatsApp turned into an essential wellspring of information and data, outperforming conventional news sources. The stage's part in data dispersal during races and social developments highlighted its effect on molding general assessment and working with grassroots getting sorted out.

Be that as it may, WhatsApp's effect on political elements likewise raised worries about the spread of deception and the potential for the stage to be taken advantage of for loathsome purposes. The application's start to finish encryption, while an aid for client protection, likewise made it trying to screen and check the spread of bogus data. WhatsApp has wrestled with tending to these difficulties, presenting highlights like message sending limits and naming sent messages to control the viral spread of falsehood.

WhatsApp's securing by Facebook in 2014 denoted a critical achievement in its excursion and brought the two open doors and difficulties. While the procurement filled the application's development and mix with the more extensive Facebook environment, it additionally brought up issues about information protection and the potential for client information to be shared across stages. The harmony between offering customized types of assistance and protecting client security turned into a focal topic in conversations encompassing WhatsApp and other Facebook-possessed properties.

The coordination of WhatsApp with other Facebook administrations, like Instagram and Facebook Courier, flagged a move towards a brought together informing foundation. This coordination expected to empower cross-stage correspondence, permitting clients on various Facebook-possessed applications to impart consistently. While introducing a more durable client experience, this coordination likewise ignited banters about client protection, information sharing, and antitrust worries.

The presentation of WhatsApp Status in 2017 added another aspect to the application's usefulness, permitting clients to share mixed media refreshes that vanish following 24 hours. This element, suggestive of Snapchat Stories, added to the pattern of transient substance and gave clients an inventive source for sharing minutes from their day to day routines. The progress of WhatsApp Status mirrored the advancing idea of content partaking in the computerized age.

WhatsApp's impact on language and correspondence standards is outstanding also. The application's UI, with its blue ticks demonstrating message read status, acquainted new layers of subtlety with advanced discussions. The utilization of emoticons, GIFs, and stickers became fundamental to communicating feelings and adding setting to messages. Truncations and web shoptalk, currently predominant in computerized correspondence, found a characteristic home inside the casual and quick fire trades on WhatsApp.

The Coronavirus pandemic in 2020 highlighted the application's importance as a device for far off correspondence and virtual association. With lockdowns and social removing estimates set up, people went to WhatsApp for remaining associated with loved ones, leading virtual get-togethers, and sharing updates. Video approaches WhatsApp turned into a life saver for those unfit to meet face to face, featuring the application's job in encouraging a feeling of progression and association during testing times.

WhatsApp's part in molding current correspondence elements is a demonstration of its flexibility and responsiveness to client needs. The application's excursion from a basic informing stage to an extensive specialized instrument mirrors its capacity to develop with changing innovative scenes and cultural assumptions. As it keeps on assuming a focal part in interfacing individuals worldwide, WhatsApp's effect on the manner in which people impart and construct connections stays a convincing account in the more extensive story of computerized correspondence.

Chapter 2

The User Experience Revolution

The Client Experience (UX) Upset has been an extraordinary power in the realm of plan and innovation. Throughout the course of recent many years, we have seen a seismic change in how clients connect with computerized items and administrations. Gone are the times of cumbersome connection points and disappointing client ventures. Today, the attention is on making consistent, natural, and superb encounters that make clients want more and more.

At the core of the UX Unrest is a central comprehension of human way of behaving and brain science. Planners and designers are at this point not simply making points of interaction; they are caretakers of client encounters. This change in outlook has impelled the business forward, prompting developments that focus on the requirements and inclinations of clients.

One of the critical drivers of the UX Insurgency is the ascent of versatile innovation. The universality of cell phones has essentially changed how individuals access data and draw in with the computerized world. Subsequently, originators have needed to adjust their way to deal with oblige the imperatives and chances of versatile stages. Responsive plan, contact motions, and portable first reasoning have become fundamental parts of the cutting edge plan toolbox.

Availability has likewise become the dominant focal point in the UX Unrest. Planning for inclusivity implies considering clients of all capacities and guaranteeing that computerized encounters are available to everybody. This goes past following legitimate necessities; about making items are really client driven. Accordingly, the plan local area has become more sensitive to the assorted necessities of clients, prompting more comprehensive and easy to use items.

The appearance of man-made consciousness (simulated intelligence) has additionally sped up the UX Unrest. AI calculations are driving keen points of interaction that adjust to client conduct, giving customized encounters that vibe tailor-made. From suggestion motors to chatbots, computer based intelligence is reshaping the way that clients associate with advanced items, making communications more regular and proficient.

Client research has turned into a foundation of the UX Insurgency. Plan choices are not generally founded on suspicions or premonitions; they are grounded in information and experiences got from client testing, reviews, and examination. This client driven approach guarantees that items are outwardly engaging as well as meet the utilitarian requirements of the ideal interest group.

Joint effort is one more sign of the UX Upset. Planners, engineers, advertisers, and different partners currently cooperate in cross-utilitarian groups, separating storehouses and encouraging a comprehensive way to deal with item improvement. This cooperative outlook guarantees that each part of the client experience is thought of, from the main connection with a promoting site to the last snap in a UI.

In the domain of web based business, the UX Upset has been especially significant. The shift from actual retail facades to web based shopping has constrained organizations to reexamine how they present their items and draw in with clients. The web based shopping experience is presently not just about making a buy; it's tied in with making a consistent and pleasant excursion from revelation to checkout.

Online entertainment stages have likewise assumed an essential part in molding the UX scene. The consistent stream of content and the requirement for moment satisfaction have impacted how points of interaction are planned. Looking over, swiping, and tapping have become natural to clients, and originators have adjusted by making points of interaction that vibe instinctive and receptive to these signals.

The UX Upset isn't restricted to the computerized domain; it has penetrated the actual world too. From the format of retail spaces to the plan of brilliant home gadgets, the standards of client focused plan are being applied to make more agreeable and effective actual encounters. The limit between the advanced and actual domains is turning out to be progressively obscured as items consistently incorporate into clients' lives.

As the UX Upheaval keeps on developing, moral contemplations have come to the front. Originators are wrestling with inquiries of protection, assent, and the unseen side-effects of their manifestations. The obligation to configuration morally is presently viewed as a center principle of the calling, with a developing accentuation on straightforwardness and client strengthening.

The democratization of configuration devices plays likewise had an impact in the UX Unrest. The hindrance to passage for hopeful fashioners has been essentially brought down, permitting a more different scope of voices to add to the plan scene. This democratization has prompted a more extravagant embroidery of plan viewpoints and a more comprehensive industry.

Looking forward, the UX Upheaval indicates that things are not pulling back. Arising advancements like increased reality (AR) and computer generated reality (VR) are ready to additionally reclassify how clients communicate with advanced content. The test for architects is to remain on the ball, expecting the requirements and assumptions for clients in a steadily developing mechanical scene.

All in all, the Client Experience Upset has been an extraordinary power that has reshaped how we connect with the computerized and actual universes. From the ascent of portable innovation to the effect of man-made consciousness, each part of the client experience has been moved by this upset. As planners keep on pushing the limits of what is conceivable, the emphasis stays on making encounters that are easy to understand as well as genuinely client driven. The excursion is continuous, and what's in store guarantees considerably additional astonishing advancements in the consistently developing field of client experience plan.

2.1 User-friendly design and accessibility of WhatsApp

Easy to understand plan and openness are basic components in the progress of any computerized stage, and WhatsApp remains as a great representation of how these standards can be successfully executed to make a broadly embraced and comprehensive specialized device. As one of the most famous informing applications internationally, WhatsApp has constantly developed its point of interaction and highlights to focus on client experience while likewise guaranteeing openness for a different client base.

At the center of WhatsApp's prosperity is its obligation to effortlessness and convenience. The UI is perfect and instinctive, permitting clients to get a handle on the application's functionalities rapidly. From sending instant messages to sharing sight and sound substance, the plan focuses on clear route, making it available to people of changing mechanical proficiency levels.

WhatsApp's plan theory rotates around giving a consistent and effective correspondence experience. The talk connection point is clear, with a recognizable design that mirrors conventional text informing.

Clients can without much of a stretch explore through individual and gathering visits, working with easy correspondence. The choice to keep the plan basic and cleaned up has added to the application's inescapable reception across age gatherings and socioeconomics.

The informing stage likewise succeeds in giving a scope of highlights without overpowering clients. Whether it's sending voice messages, sharing pictures and recordings, or settling on voice and video decisions, WhatsApp consistently coordinates these functionalities into the UI. The application's prosperity lies in finding some kind of harmony between offering a far reaching set of highlights and keeping an easy to use interface that doesn't threaten or befuddle clients.

A prominent part of WhatsApp's easy to use configuration is its obligation to stage consistency. Whether clients access the application on Android or iOS, the experience remains astoundingly comparative. This consistency in plan and usefulness encourages a feeling of commonality, lessening the expectation to learn and adapt for clients exchanging between various gadgets or working frameworks. This approach adds to a positive client experience and energizes client maintenance.

Openness is a guiding principle implanted in WhatsApp's plan ethos. Perceiving the different necessities of its client base, the stage has carried out highlights that take care of people with shifting capacities. One such element is the choice to increment text dimension inside talks, obliging clients with visual impedances. Moreover, WhatsApp upholds VoiceOver on iOS and TalkBack on Android, guaranteeing that the application is traversable for people who depend on screen perusers.

The obligation to openness stretches out to media content also. WhatsApp permits clients to add alt text to pictures, giving a text based portrayal of the visual substance. This component is especially gainful for clients with visual impedances, empowering them to comprehend and draw in with shared pictures. By consolidating these availability highlights, WhatsApp endeavors to make its foundation comprehensive and inviting to clients with different necessities.

WhatsApp's easy to understand plan and openness endeavors are not restricted to the application's center functionalities; they additionally stretch out to the onboarding system. The enlistment and arrangement process is intended in all honestly, directing clients through the essential strides without pointless confusions. This straightforwardness in onboarding adds to the stage's allure, particularly in locales with assorted client socioeconomics and fluctuating degrees of mechanical commonality.

Notwithstanding visual openness highlights, WhatsApp puts areas of strength for an on semantic variety. The application upholds a large number of dialects, permitting clients to impart in their favored language. This obligation to phonetic inclusivity is pivotal in a worldwide setting, where clients from various districts and semantic foundations meet up on the stage.

The easy to understand plan of WhatsApp is additionally exemplified in its security and protection highlights. While these perspectives may not be quickly noticeable in the UI, their mix is critical to laying out trust and guaranteeing a positive client experience. WhatsApp utilizes start to finish encryption for messages, guaranteeing that main the expected beneficiary can get to the substance. This obligation to client protection lines up with contemporary client assumptions and adds to the stage's standing as a safe specialized device.

WhatsApp's UI is likewise intended to focus on fundamental highlights, adding to a smoothed out and centered insight. For example, the visit list noticeably shows late discussions, making it simple for clients to get to their most continuous contacts. Furthermore, the position of elements, for example, notices and calls is natural, adding to a durable and client driven plan.

The stage's obligation to easy to understand configuration is apparent in its responsiveness to client criticism. WhatsApp consistently refreshes its application, presenting new highlights and refining existing ones in view of client input. This iterative way to deal with configuration guarantees that the stage stays lined up with developing client assumptions and innovative headways. It likewise shows a readiness to adjust and improve, a vital viewpoint in the quickly changing scene of computerized correspondence.

WhatsApp's prosperity isn't exclusively credited to its plan; its availability likewise reaches out to the reasonableness of the help. The stage works on a model where clients can send instant messages, settle on voice and video decisions, and offer mixed media content utilizing web information as opposed to conventional SMS or call charges. This approach democratizes admittance to specialized devices, particularly in locales where the expense of customary correspondence administrations can be a hindrance.

The obligation to availability and easy to use configuration is especially clear in WhatsApp's endeavors to connect the computerized partition. In districts with restricted web network, WhatsApp has presented highlights like WhatsApp Web, permitting clients to get to the stage through a PC. This not just takes care of clients who might have restricted admittance to cell phones yet additionally upgrades the general availability of the stage.

WhatsApp's example of overcoming adversity highlights the significance of a client driven approach in the plan and improvement of computerized stages. By focusing on straightforwardness, consistency, and openness, WhatsApp has made a specialized instrument that reverberates with a different and worldwide client base. The application's development mirrors a comprehension of client needs and a promise to refining the client experience ceaselessly.

As innovation proceeds to progress, and client assumptions develop, WhatsApp's way to deal with easy to understand plan and openness fills in as a benchmark for other computerized stages.

The illustrations gained from WhatsApp's prosperity stress the meaning of setting clients at the focal point of the plan cycle, guaranteeing that innovation stays a device that upgrades, instead of upsets, the human experience.

2.2 Impact of intuitive interfaces on global user adoption

The effect of natural connection points on worldwide client reception has been absolutely progressive, reshaping the manner in which people communicate with computerized items and administrations across the globe. The expression "instinctive connection point" alludes to a UI plan that is so easy to use and regular that clients can undoubtedly comprehend and explore the framework without the requirement for broad preparation or guidelines. As innovation has become progressively incorporated into our regular routines, the significance of instinctive points of interaction has developed dramatically, affecting the achievement and inescapable reception of different computerized stages.

At the core of the instinctive point of interaction peculiarity is the idea of client experience (UX). Client experience envelops the general collaboration a client has with an item or administration, including parts of ease of use, openness, and fulfillment. Instinctive points of interaction focus on a positive client experience by limiting mental burden and establishing a climate where clients can achieve undertakings easily and productivity.

One of the critical drivers of the natural connection point upheaval is the ascent of cell phones and touchscreen gadgets. The coming of the iPhone in 2007 denoted an essential crossroads throughout the entire existence of UIs, presenting a touch-based interface that was natural and responsive. The capacity to swipe, tap, and squeeze to associate with computerized content changed the manner in which clients drew in with innovation. Accordingly, instinctive points of interaction became inseparable from the touchscreen experience, setting new principles for client assumptions.

The progress of stages like Apple's iOS and Google's Android, the two of which focus on natural plan standards, plays had a huge impact in molding the worldwide scene of client reception. Versatile working frameworks have turned into the doorway to a large number of utilizations and administrations, and the instinctive idea of these points of interaction has added to the broad reception of cell phones across different socioeconomics and districts.

In the domain of web based business, natural connection points have been instrumental in molding client conduct and driving worldwide reception. Stages like Amazon have set the norm for consistent internet shopping encounters. The capacity to peruse items easily, add things to a truck, and complete a buy with a couple of taps has changed the manner in which individuals shop. Instinctive points of interaction have made internet shopping additional open as well as impacted the progress from conventional physical retail to computerized trade on a worldwide scale.

Online entertainment stages, one more foundation of the advanced scene, owe a lot of their prosperity to instinctive connection points. From the beginning of Facebook to the quick ascent of Instagram and TikTok, the capacity to scroll, similar to, remark, and offer substance with negligible exertion has been a main thrust in client reception. The instinctive plan of these stages takes care of a different client base, rising above age, language, and mechanical capability.

The effect of instinctive connection points isn't restricted to buyer confronting applications; it reaches out to big business programming also. In the corporate world, where time is frequently of the pith, natural connection points smooth out complex work processes and increment efficiency. Undertaking asset arranging (ERP) frameworks, client relationship the executives (CRM) apparatuses, and cooperative stages have all embraced natural plan standards to upgrade client reception inside associations.

Cloud-based administrations address another space where natural connection points play had a critical impact in worldwide reception. Stages like Google Drive and Dropbox have improved on document capacity and sharing, making it simple for clients to team up across lines and time regions. The instinctive idea of these connection points has brought hindrances down to section for clients with changing degrees of specialized mastery, cultivating a more comprehensive computerized climate.

The effect of natural connection points on worldwide client reception is intently attached to the democratization of innovation. As advanced items and administrations become more open, the client base grows past well informed early adopters to incorporate people from different foundations and socioeconomics. This inclusivity is clear in the manner natural connection points take special care of clients with fluctuating degrees of mechanical proficiency, separating obstructions and making innovation more agreeable.

The outcome of natural points of interaction is additionally entwined with the brain research of client conduct. Human-PC communication research has reliably exhibited that clients lean toward interfaces that line up with their psychological models and assumptions. Instinctive connection points influence recognizable examples and similitudes, diminishing the mental exertion expected for clients to comprehend and cooperate with a framework. This lines up with the mental guideline of mental familiarity, where individuals will generally favor undertakings that are straightforward and execute.

Voice interfaces address one more wilderness in the development of natural connection points. Remote helpers like Amazon's Alexa, Apple's Siri, and find out about Aide have carried normal language cooperation to the very front. Clients can clarify some pressing issues, set updates, and control shrewd gadgets utilizing voice orders, making a more natural and conversational connection point. This shift towards voice interfaces mirrors a more profound comprehension of client inclinations and a craving for interfaces that reflect certifiable correspondence.

The impact of natural points of interaction on worldwide client reception stretches out to the domain of wellbeing and health applications. As wellness trackers and wellbeing observing gadgets have become omnipresent, the convenience and instinct of these connection points have been pivotal in empowering people to take on and support solid propensities. From following everyday moves toward checking rest designs, natural points of interaction add to a positive client experience, persuading clients to draw in with their wellbeing and prosperity.

Schooling innovation, or EdTech, is another area where instinctive connection points have made critical advances. As computerized learning stages become more common, the requirement for interfaces that work with viable correspondence and commitment has developed. Natural plan standards in instructive applications and stages assist students of any age with exploring content, complete tasks, and take part in intelligent exercises with negligible contact.

The impact of natural connection points on worldwide client reception isn't without its difficulties. As innovation propels, the interest for additional modern highlights and functionalities develops. Adjusting the requirement for advancement with the basic to keep up with straightforwardness and instinct is quite difficult for creators and designers. Finding some kind of harmony is vital to guarantee that clients can profit from new highlights without forfeiting the usability that characterizes natural connection points.

The job of social variety in forming natural connection points couldn't possibly be more significant. As computerized stages plan to contact a worldwide crowd, contemplations of social standards, language inclinations, and plan feel become foremost. Adjusting connection points to resound with different social foundations adds to a more comprehensive and universally acknowledged client experience.

With regards to the Web of Things (IoT), where gadgets and frameworks are interconnected, the significance of instinctive points of interaction turns out to be much more articulated. As clients communicate with a bunch of shrewd gadgets, from indoor regulators to fridges, the test lies in making connection points that fit the client experience across these different endpoints. Natural plan turns into a binding together consider the perplexing environment of interconnected gadgets.

The eventual fate of natural connection points is probably going to be formed by arising advances like increased reality (AR) and augmented reality (VR). These vivid advances present additional opportunities for collaboration and commitment. Planning instinctive connection points for AR and VR conditions requires a nuanced comprehension of spatial collaborations and client conduct, introducing the two difficulties and potential open doors for the plan local area.

All in all, the effect of natural connection points on worldwide client reception is a diverse peculiarity that traverses businesses and advances. From the ascent of touchscreen gadgets to the coordination of voice interfaces and the globalization of advanced stages, natural plan standards have become vital to the progress of computerized items and administrations. As innovation keeps on advancing, the test stays for planners and engineers to offset advancement with straightforwardness, guaranteeing that natural connection points stay at the very front of client driven plan. The continuous journey for consistent, easy to use connections isn't just a demonstration of the past outcome of natural connection points yet in addition a compass directing the way forward in a steadily changing computerized scene.

2.3 Cultural implications of WhatsApp's commitment to simplicity

WhatsApp's obligation to effortlessness has had significant social ramifications, impacting the manner in which individuals impart, associate, and offer data on a worldwide scale. As one of the most broadly utilized informing applications, WhatsApp's easy to understand configuration has risen above social limits, making it available and interesting to different populaces. Analyzing the social ramifications of WhatsApp's obligation to effortlessness uncovers not exclusively its effect on correspondence designs yet additionally its part in forming social associations, cultivating network, and adding to the development of social standards in the computerized age.

At the center of WhatsApp's social effect is its natural UI. The application's plan focuses on straightforwardness, guaranteeing that clients, no matter what their mechanical capability, can undoubtedly explore and use its elements. This obligation to a clear client experience has democratized admittance to computerized correspondence, arriving at clients in districts with shifting degrees of mechanical framework and proficiency.

In many societies, the demonstration of correspondence holds critical social and individual worth. WhatsApp's straightforwardness has smoothed out this cycle, permitting clients to trade instant messages, interactive media content, and settle on voice and video decisions with insignificant exertion. The application's plan reflects the effortlessness of customary text informing, making the change to computerized correspondence consistent for clients acclimated with additional simple types of collaboration.

The social ramifications of WhatsApp's effortlessness are especially apparent in locales where admittance to cell phones and computerized specialized apparatuses has quickly expanded. In emerging nations, where cell phones act as essential specialized gadgets, WhatsApp has turned into an omnipresent stage for remaining associated with loved ones. The application's straightforwardness adds to its openness, empowering clients with fluctuating degrees of mechanical commonality to easily take part in computerized correspondence.

WhatsApp's part in protecting and changing social correspondence standards is essential. The application upholds a large number of dialects, permitting clients to impart in their local tongue. This etymological inclusivity is essential in areas described by phonetic variety, where people can put themselves out there serenely in their favored language. By working with correspondence in numerous dialects, WhatsApp obliges social subtleties and encourages a feeling of having a place among clients.

Past language, WhatsApp's obligation to effortlessness reaches out to the plan of expressive highlights, like emoticons and stickers. Emoticons, specifically, have turned into a general language that rises above phonetic and social obstructions. The straightforwardness and visual allure of emoticons make them a useful asset for conveying feelings and articulations, encouraging a more nuanced and socially touchy type of computerized correspondence.

The effortlessness of WhatsApp likewise assumes a part in reshaping social elements inside families and networks. Bunch talks, an unmistakable component of the application, empower clients to remain associated with different individuals at the same time. This has critical social ramifications, especially in societies that accentuate public ties and aggregate correspondence. WhatsApp bunches act as computerized augmentations of familial and local area organizations, considering the trading of data, coordination of occasions, and the sharing of social practices.

In certain societies, WhatsApp has turned into a stage for the dispersal of information and data. The effortlessness of the application works with the fast spread of messages, including news updates, declarations, and far-reaching developments. Notwithstanding, this simplicity of data dispersal likewise raises worries about the spread of falsehood, as socially critical messages can be shared without appropriate check. The social ramifications of WhatsApp's effortlessness in this setting feature the requirement for advanced education and mindful correspondence rehearses.

The straightforwardness of WhatsApp is especially significant in societies where various leveled correspondence standards win. In conventional social orders with unmistakable power structures, the straightforwardness of the application cultivates more libertarian correspondence designs. The capacity to send messages, settle on decisions, and offer substance with negligible convention evens the odds, empowering people across various social layers to take part in immediate and casual correspondence.

WhatsApp's obligation to effortlessness lines up with the more extensive pattern of computerized stages becoming necessary to the social texture of social orders. In many societies, the trading of good tidings, warm words, and festivities has progressed from conventional mediums to advanced stages. WhatsApp's straightforwardness in sending media content, like pictures and recordings, works with the sharing of social celebrations and individual achievements, supporting the application's job as a social connector.

The ascent of WhatsApp as an essential specialized device has likewise impacted dating and close connections in different societies. The straightforwardness of the application permits couples to remain associated easily, regardless of geological distances. The trading of messages, voice notes, and mixed media content improves the closeness of remote relationships, adding to the advancement of computerized romance standards.

WhatsApp's social effect reaches out to the working environment, where the application's effortlessness has changed proficient correspondence designs. In societies where progressive designs are predominant, the application gives a stage to more straightforward and casual correspondence among partners and bosses. The effortlessness of WhatsApp bunches works with speedy coordination, independent direction, and the sharing of data inside proficient circles.

While the effortlessness of WhatsApp has without a doubt achieved positive social changes, it isn't without its difficulties. In certain societies, the simplicity of correspondence worked with by the application has prompted the obscuring of limits among individual and expert circles. The assumption for steady accessibility on WhatsApp can add to pressure and burnout, testing laid out standards of balance between serious and fun activities in specific social settings.

The social ramifications of WhatsApp's effortlessness additionally converge with issues of security and reconnaissance. In societies where thoughts of protection differ, the application's start to finish encryption gives a layer of safety. Nonetheless, the metadata created by client cooperations, like the timing and recurrence of messages, can in any case uncover critical experiences. Exploring the harmony between the advantages of network and the protection of security stays a complex social thought.

WhatsApp's job in social articulation is additionally exemplified by its Status highlight, permitting clients to share sight and sound updates that vanish following

24 hours. This component mirrors the social shift towards fleeting substance and the longing for self-articulation. Clients influence Notices to share social encounters, commend occasions, and express imagination, adding to the dynamic and developing nature of social articulation in the advanced age.

The effortlessness of WhatsApp plays likewise had an impact in political and social developments worldwide. In locales where conventional types of media are controlled or edited, the application turns into a crucial device for dispersing data, coordinating fights, and cultivating fortitude. The straightforwardness of the stage empowers people to enhance their voices, share ongoing updates, and direction activities, adding to the democratization of correspondence in social and political settings.

In any case, the social ramifications of WhatsApp's part in political developments are not without debate. The application's encoded nature, while giving a degree of safety, has likewise been censured for empowering the spread of falsehood and fanatic belief systems.

The straightforwardness of message sending, an element intended for simple sharing, has been taken advantage of in a few social and political settings to quickly scatter unsubstantiated data.

WhatsApp's obligation to effortlessness is additionally reflected in its protection from jumbling the connection point with promotions. Dissimilar to other web-based entertainment stages, WhatsApp has kept a more moderate way to deal with adaptation. This choice lines up with social inclinations for subtle correspondence and adds to the application's allure as a space for individual and credible communications.

As WhatsApp keeps on developing, its effect on social standards will probably extend. The application's obligation to effortlessness positions it as a social power that shapes the manner in which people impart, put themselves out there, and associate with others. The continuous test lies in adjusting the positive parts of network and social trade with the requirement for mindful computerized citizenship, security, and the relief of possible adverse results.

All in all, WhatsApp's obligation to straightforwardness has expansive social ramifications, affecting the manner in which individuals convey, associate, and put themselves out there in assorted social orders all over the planet. The application's natural plan has democratized advanced correspondence, making it available across various societies and socioeconomics. From reshaping social elements inside families to changing proficient correspondence designs, WhatsApp's effect on social standards is multi-layered. As the application keeps on developing, its job as a social connector and powerhouse features the multifaceted exchange between innovation, effortlessness, and the texture of human culture in the computerized age.

Chapter 3

Breaking Down Borders

Mechanical headways assumed a crucial part in this significant shift. The quick advancement of man-made consciousness, quantum processing, and biotechnology had raised's comprehension humankind might interpret the universe as well as disintegrated the hindrances that once restricted people to explicit geological areas. The advanced domain turned into a multifaceted woven artwork, entwining the narratives of individuals from each side of the globe.

The rise of a brought together worldwide cognizance denoted a takeoff from the ethnocentric belief systems that had powered clashes for quite a long time. The incorporation of different points of view turned into a wellspring of solidarity, as the aggregate insight of mankind was tackled to address squeezing difficulties. No longer did countries contend in a lose situation; all things being equal, joint effort turned into the foundation of progress.

One of the main appearances of this borderless world was the development of training. Virtual homerooms, controlled by vivid advancements, permitted understudies to associate with guides and companions across landmasses. The trading of thoughts became unfathomable, as social trade programs rose above the limits of actual nearness. The once unrealistic walls of obliviousness disintegrated, leading to an age that esteemed grasping over bias.

In this borderless future, the idea of citizenship went through an extreme change. Ethnicity turned out to be to a lesser extent a characterizing factor, and worldwide citizenship came first. The world's occupants perceived their common obligation regarding the planet's prosperity, encouraging a feeling of interconnectedness that rose above international limits. Natural difficulties, when seen through the tight focal point of public interest, turned into an energizing point for aggregate activity.

The monetary scene likewise encountered a seismic shift. The customary models of exchange and trade, frequently impeded by protectionism and patriotism, gave way to a more liquid and comprehensive worldwide economy. Blockchain innovation worked with straightforward and decentralized exchanges, destroying the requirement for middle people and encouraging trust across borders. Asset dispersion turned out to be more impartial, with an emphasis on manageable improvement that focused on the requirements of both present and people in the future.

Medical care, as well, went through a transformation in this borderless world. Propels in clinical examination were shared transparently, speeding up the improvement of fixes and medicines for once-crippling sicknesses. Telemedicine overcame any barrier among patients and medical care suppliers, guaranteeing that quality clinical consideration was available to all, paying little mind to geological area. The destruction of pandemics turned into a worldwide undertaking, with countries pooling assets and skill to face wellbeing emergencies on the whole.

As lines broke down, so did the divisions between the advanced and actual domains. Increased reality turned into a vital piece of day to day existence, flawlessly mixing the virtual and unmistakable universes. Correspondence rose above phonetic obstructions through ongoing interpretation innovations, encouraging a genuinely worldwide discussion. The lavishness of social variety was commended, as people investigated and embraced the customs and points of view of others.

The political scene, as well, saw a change. Customary thoughts of power gave way to another worldview of worldwide administration. Worldwide foundations advanced to mirror the interconnected idea of contemporary difficulties. Tact turned into a cooperative undertaking, with countries cooperating to resolve issues, for example, environmental change, neediness, and basic freedoms. The once inflexible lines between country states became permeable, taking into account the free progression of thoughts, assets, and ability.

The idea of safety went through a significant reexamination in this borderless world. Rather than building walls, countries put resources into cooperative endeavors to address the main drivers of contention. Demilitarization drives built up some momentum, and the center moved from military could to conciliatory arrangements. Worldwide security turned into a common obligation, with countries contributing their mastery to keep up with harmony and strength on a planetary scale.

Artistic expressions prospered in this borderless period, drawing motivation from the horde societies that crossed and consolidated. Imaginative articulations rose above customary limits, leading to a worldwide social embroidery that mirrored the common human experience. Craftsmen teamed up across mainlands, improving their work with different impacts and points of view. The limits among classes and mediums obscured, making a combination of creative articulation that reverberated with individuals all over the planet.

The shift towards a borderless world was not without challenges. Protection from change, energized by wistfulness for the natural, took steps to block progress. Well established biases and power irregular characteristics waited, requiring a deliberate work to destroy. Notwithstanding, the aggregate will of mankind demonstrated versatile, and another ethos arose — one that embraced the interconnectedness of all life on The planet.

Schooling assumed a vital part in destroying the psychological boundaries that obstructed advancement. Educational programs were upgraded to accentuate decisive reasoning, sympathy, and worldwide mindfulness. Understudies were presented to a different scope of viewpoints, testing their suppositions and cultivating a feeling of interest on the planet past their nearby environmental elements. The thought of a solitary, fixed character gave way to a more liquid comprehension of self, formed by the crossing points of culture, history, and individual encounters.

In the domain of innovation, moral contemplations became the dominant focal point. As man-made consciousness and biotechnology progressed, the requirement for mindful development became central. Worldwide principles were laid out to guarantee the moral turn of events and utilization of arising advances, forestalling their abuse and relieving likely dangers. The cooperative idea of mechanical advancement mirrored the common obligation to tackle development to assist all humankind.

Monetary frameworks went through a significant change to address the variations that had endured in past times. Abundance reallocation measures were carried out on a worldwide scale, guaranteeing that the advantages of monetary development arrived at all sides of the world. The center moved from Gross domestic product as the sole measurement of progress to a more all encompassing methodology that thought about ecological manageability, social prosperity, and evenhanded circulation of assets.

Medical services turned into a general right, with a promise to giving admittance to quality clinical consideration for all. Innovative work endeavors were cooperative, with an emphasis on tending to the wellbeing needs of the whole worldwide populace. Preventive measures and early mediations came first, prompting a huge improvement in generally wellbeing results.

The disintegration of customary lines likewise ignited a reconsideration of social characters. As opposed to review variety as a danger, individuals praised the extravagance it brought to their lives. Social trade programs prospered, encouraging shared understanding and appreciation. Human expressions assumed a significant part in this social renaissance, filling in as a scaffold between various networks and giving a stage to shared articulations of mankind.

In the political field, the idea of public interest went through an extreme shift. Pioneers perceived that the difficulties confronting humankind — whether ecological, monetary, or social — rose above borders. Worldwide collaboration turned into the standard, with countries pooling their assets and mastery to address worldwide difficulties. The Unified Countries developed into a more successful and comprehensive establishment, filling in as a stage for conciliatory exchange and aggregate activity.

Security standards additionally advanced to mirror the interconnected idea of contemporary difficulties. The accentuation moved from military could to preventive strategy, compromise, and tending to the main drivers of weakness. Countries put resources into practical improvement drives that handled issues like destitution, disparity, and ecological debasement, perceiving that an additional fair and evenhanded world was innately safer.

Regardless of these positive changes, the way to a borderless world was not without hindrances. The remnants of old belief systems and power structures opposed change, gripping to obsolete thoughts of patriotism and selectiveness. Notwithstanding, the aggregate will of the worldwide populace won, as people, networks, and countries cooperated to beat these difficulties.

The borderless universe of 2100 was a demonstration of the flexibility and versatility of humankind. It was an existence where the examples of history had been regarded, and the mix-ups of the past were not rehashed. It was a reality where the hindrances that once partitioned individuals had disintegrated, leading to a worldwide local area limited by a common obligation to a superior future.

In this borderless world, the human soul took off higher than ever. Liberated from the imperatives of thin personalities and restricted points of view, people embraced their interconnectedness with the more extensive embroidered artwork of mankind. It was a reality where the aggregate insight of different societies, narratives, and encounters united to shape a future that was genuinely shared by all.

The excursion to a borderless world was not a straight movement. It required deliberate endeavors, penances, and an aggregate obligation to values that rose above tight personal circumstance. It requested a change in outlook in how people and social orders apparent themselves and their spot on the planet. The excursion was set apart by snapshots of win and difficulties, yet the objective — a world without borders — filled in as an encouraging sign and motivation.

3.1 Cross-cultural communication facilitated by WhatsApp

In the developing scene of the 21st hundred years, correspondence has risen above conventional limits, introducing a time where worldwide network isn't simply an extravagance yet a need. Among the heap instruments that work with this interconnectedness, WhatsApp stands apart as a strong stage that has re-imagined culturally diverse correspondence. With north of two billion month to month clients around the world, the application has turned into a universal power in crossing over holes, cultivating understanding, and associating individuals from different foundations.

At the core of WhatsApp's effect on diverse correspondence is its effortlessness and openness. The stage's easy to understand interface, combined with its accessibility on cell phones, has democratized correspondence on a worldwide scale. At this point not bound to the domain of messages or conventional instant messages, people from various corners of the world can now take part progressively discussions with the tap of a finger. This promptness has broken down transient and spatial hindrances, empowering moment correspondence regardless of topographical distances.

One of WhatsApp's outstanding highlights is its help for sight and sound components. Past plain message, clients can share pictures, recordings, voice messages, and archives consistently. This sight and sound capacity adds a rich layer to multifaceted correspondence, permitting people to communicate their thoughts in different ways. Visual components rise above semantic contrasts, empowering clients to convey feelings, share encounters, and exhibit their social subtleties from the perspective of pictures and recordings.

Besides, the application's voice informing highlight has demonstrated instrumental in beating language hindrances. In this present reality where semantic variety is a main trait, the capacity to convey through verbally expressed word works with a more profound comprehension between people from various social foundations. The subtleties of tone, inflection, and articulation convey importance past the imperatives of composed text, encouraging a more valid and nuanced type of culturally diverse exchange.

WhatsApp's part in separating language obstructions stretches out past voice messages. The stage upholds continuous language interpretation, empowering clients to impart flawlessly regardless of whether they communicate in various dialects. This element is especially important in diverse settings, where people may not share a typical language. The straightforwardness with which clients can decipher messages improves the inclusivity of discussions, permitting individuals to take part in significant trades without the deterrent of phonetic restrictions.

In the domain of business and expert correspondence, WhatsApp has arisen as an imperative device for diverse coordinated effort. The stage's gathering visit highlight works with conversations and decision-production among geologically scattered groups.

Organizations can use this usefulness to interface representatives, clients, and accomplices across borders, encouraging a cooperative climate that rises above the limits of customary office spaces.

Past text-based correspondence, WhatsApp's video calling highlight has turned into a key part in keeping up with relational associations across societies. The capacity to see and hear far off companions, relatives, or partners continuously adds a layer of closeness to diverse connections. This visual association is particularly huge in a time where actual travel might be compelled, permitting people to keep a feeling of closeness in spite of geological distances.

WhatsApp's effect on diverse correspondence isn't restricted to individual collaborations; it stretches out to local area building and social developments. The application fills in as an impetus for the development of virtual networks that rise above public boundaries. These people group, joined by shared interests, objectives, or personalities, influence WhatsApp's gathering talk highlights to interface similar people across societies, encouraging a feeling of having a place that rises above geological requirements.

Nonetheless, the pervasiveness and comfort of WhatsApp additionally raise significant contemplations with respect to protection and security in diverse correspondence.

As people share individual stories, pictures, and touchy data, the requirement for strong protection measures becomes central. WhatsApp has executed start to finish encryption to safeguard client information, guaranteeing that messages stay private and secure. By the by, the advancing scene of computerized correspondence requires consistent endeavors to upgrade safety efforts and address arising difficulties.

In the instructive circle, WhatsApp has arisen as a unique device for multifaceted learning and coordinated effort. Understudies and teachers from various areas of the planet can take part progressively conversations, share assets, and team up on projects consistently. This globalized way to deal with instruction encourages a more profound comprehension of different viewpoints, planning people for a reality where intercultural capability is a fundamental expertise.

WhatsApp's effect on diverse correspondence reaches out to the domain of medical care too. Telemedicine, worked with by the stage, empowers people to talk with medical services experts across borders, conquering geological limitations and expanding admittance to clinical mastery. The quickness of correspondence on WhatsApp demonstrates basic in crisis circumstances, where ideal exhortation or mediation can have a huge effect in results.

While WhatsApp has evidently changed multifaceted correspondence, it is fundamental to recognize the difficulties and contemplations that go with this change. The computerized partition, set apart by variations in admittance to innovation and the web, stays a boundary to worldwide network. Addressing these incongruities requires a purposeful work to guarantee that the advantages of stages like WhatsApp are open to all, paying little mind to financial variables.

Besides, the potential for deception and the spread of unsafe substance on stages like WhatsApp highlight the requirement for advanced education and mindful use. The application's start to finish encryption, while significant for security, additionally presents difficulties regarding content balance. Finding some kind of harmony among protection and forestalling the abuse of the stage is a continuous test that requires joint effort between innovation organizations, policymakers, and clients.

As we explore the intricacies of multifaceted correspondence worked with by WhatsApp, perceiving the groundbreaking capability of this technology is basic. The stage has turned into a virtual scaffold, interfacing people, networks, and societies in manners that were once impossible. It has democratized correspondence, enabled people to share their accounts on a worldwide stage, and worked with a more interconnected world.

All in all, WhatsApp's effect on culturally diverse correspondence is significant and multi-layered. The stage's availability, sight and sound capacities, language interpretation highlights, and constant specialized devices have changed the way people, organizations, and networks communicate across borders. While difficulties, for example, protection concerns and the computerized partition persevere, the positive commitments of WhatsApp to cultivating figuring out, joint effort, and association in a borderless world couldn't possibly be more significant. As innovation keeps on developing, so too will the manners by which WhatsApp and comparable stages shape the scene of multifaceted correspondence, assuming a crucial part in building spans across different societies and cultivating a more interconnected worldwide local area.

3.2 Language barriers and how the platform addresses them

In a world that is progressively interconnected, language obstructions present critical difficulties to successful correspondence. These hindrances can obstruct coordinated effort, limit admittance to data, and hinder the trading of thoughts across societies. Notwithstanding, mechanical headways have given answers for relieve these difficulties, and one stage that plays made light of a vital part in breaking language obstructions is Google Decipher.

Language obstructions are multi-layered, stretching out past simple phonetic contrasts to incorporate social subtleties, colloquial articulations, and relevant implications. They can appear in different situations, from regular discussions to global transactions, making snags that impede the free progression of data and understanding. As the worldwide local area turns out to be more reliant, tending to language obstructions is fundamental for encouraging significant associations and cooperation.

Google Interpret, created by Google, is an internet based interpretation administration that expects to connect language holes by giving moment interpretations between various dialects. At first sent off in 2006, the stage has gone through critical headways, utilizing AI and computerized reasoning to upgrade its interpretation abilities.

Today, Google Decipher upholds more than 100 dialects, making it a useful asset for people, organizations, and associations trying to conquer language hindrances in different settings.

One of the essential ways Google Decipher addresses language hindrances is through its message interpretation highlight. Clients can enter text in one language, and the stage gives a close moment interpretation into the ideal objective language. This usefulness is priceless for people imparting across semantic partitions, permitting them to comprehend and pass on messages effortlessly. From relaxed discussions to proficient correspondence, the text interpretation highlight works with correspondence in different settings.

Google Decipher's viability in tending to language hindrances is additionally enhanced by its combination with different applications and administrations. The stage's Programming interface (Application Programming Connection point) empowers engineers to incorporate interpretation abilities into their own applications, sites, and administrations. This joining expands the scope of Google Make an interpretation of, permitting clients to get to interpretation highlights flawlessly inside the setting of their favored computerized stages.

Notwithstanding text interpretation, Google Decipher offers a hearty arrangement of highlights for defeating language boundaries continuously correspondence. The stage's discussion mode permits clients to participate in communicated in discussions across dialects, with the application giving moment interpretations to the two members. This component is especially valuable in up close and personal collaborations, empowering people who communicate in various dialects to convey smoothly without the requirement for a common language.

Moreover, Google Decipher upholds the interpretation of composed text in pictures through its picture acknowledgment highlight. Clients can catch pictures containing text, like signs or archives, and the stage extricates and makes an interpretation of the text into the ideal language. This usefulness demonstrates important in circumstances where prompt interpretation of visual data is essential, improving openness and understanding.

The stage's abilities stretch out to penmanship acknowledgment, permitting clients to enter text by composing characters on their gadget's screen. This element is particularly useful for dialects with non-Latin contents, where composing on a customary console might challenge. By perceiving manually written input, Google Decipher obliges different composing frameworks, guaranteeing inclusivity in its language interpretation administrations.

Past its singular client applications, Google Decipher's effect on language obstructions is additionally clear in its commitments to worldwide openness. The stage has been instrumental in making advanced content more comprehensive by offering site interpretation administrations. Site proprietors can coordinate Google Convert into their locales, empowering guests to see content in their favored language. This element improves the openness of data, separating language hindrances for a more different and worldwide crowd.

The advancement of Google Decipher features the coordination of man-made consciousness (simulated intelligence) and AI (ML) in language interpretation. The stage's brain machine interpretation (NMT) models, presented in 2016, denoted a huge headway in interpretation exactness. NMT uses profound learning calculations to figure out the setting of a sentence, bringing about additional relevantly exact and familiar interpretations. This change in interpretation system addresses a jump forward in tending to the subtleties of language, adding to more normal and logically pertinent correspondence.

Google Make an interpretation of's introduction to voice interpretation has been one more extraordinary part of its way to deal with conquering language hindrances. The stage's discourse to-text and text-to-discourse capacities empower clients to have communicated in discussions in various dialects, with the application giving ongoing interpretations. This usefulness has boundless applications, from movement and the travel industry to worldwide conferences, working with correspondence in situations where communicated in language is the essential method of association.

In any case, recognizing the inborn difficulties in language interpretation, even with cutting edge innovations is fundamental. While Google Decipher succeeds in conveying the general significance of text and expressed words, it might experience challenges with colloquial articulations, social subtleties, or exceptionally particular phrasing. Accordingly, clients should move toward machine interpretation apparatuses with an attention to their constraints and exercise alert, especially in basic or delicate settings.

The persistent refinement of Google Decipher is a continuous cycle, with updates and enhancements pointed toward improving its exactness and growing its language capacities. The stage's dependence on client criticism and commitments assumes a urgent part in refining its calculations and tending to explicit phonetic subtleties. This iterative methodology mirrors a promise to furnishing clients with progressively dependable and nuanced interpretations, adding to more powerful multifaceted correspondence.

Google Decipher's effect on language boundaries reaches out past individual clients to incorporate instructive foundations, organizations, and non-benefit associations. In training, the stage works with language advancing by giving moment interpretations and elocution help. Understudies can utilize the stage to interpret texts, grasp new words, and practice articulation, upgrading their language obtaining experience.

In the business domain, Google Decipher fills in as a significant device for organizations working in global business sectors. It empowers associations to speak with clients, accomplices, and clients in their favored dialects, encouraging more grounded connections and working with cross-line joint efforts. The stage's coordination with business specialized devices further smoothes out culturally diverse connections, taking into consideration more proficient and viable worldwide correspondence.

Non-benefit associations and compassionate endeavors likewise benefit from Google Decipher's abilities. In emergency circumstances or during aid ventures, the stage helps correspondence between help laborers and neighborhood networks, in any event, when they communicate in various dialects. This adds to more successful coordination and backing in assorted social settings, exhibiting the capability of innovation to address language hindrances in the midst of hardship.

Notwithstanding its many benefits, Google Decipher and comparable stages brief conversations about social responsiveness and the potential for semantic homogenization. While innovation works with correspondence, it is fundamental for save and celebrate phonetic variety. Machine interpretation instruments ought to be seen as enhancements as opposed to trades for human language learning and understanding.

Besides, the moral contemplations encompassing the utilization of machine interpretation innovations come to the very front. Issues connected with protection, information security, and the dependable utilization of simulated intelligence in language interpretation require continuous examination. As these innovations become basic to multifaceted correspondence, a reasonable methodology that focuses on moral contemplations is essential for their proceeded with improvement and reception.

All in all, language boundaries are unavoidable impediments to successful correspondence in our interconnected world. Google Decipher has arisen as a useful asset in tending to these boundaries, offering arrangements that range text, voice, and picture interpretation. Its effect stretches out across different areas, from individual connections to instruction, business, and philanthropic endeavors. The stage's development, driven by progressions in computer based intelligence and AI, mirrors a promise to working on the exactness and subtlety of language interpretation.

While Google Interpret has without a doubt changed diverse correspondence, it is vital for approach its utilization with a nuanced comprehension of its capacities and restrictions. The stage, similar to any innovation, is an instrument that can improve correspondence when utilized reasonably. As we explore the developing scene of language boundaries and innovative arrangements, a smart and moral methodology guarantees that these instruments contribute decidedly to encouraging comprehension and coordinated effort across different phonetic and social settings.

3.3 WhatsApp's role in fostering a sense of global interconnectedness

In the contemporary scene of worldwide correspondence, WhatsApp has arisen as a groundbreaking power, generally modifying the way people, networks, and organizations communicate across borders. With more than two billion month to month clients, the stage has turned into a pervasive instrument, working with continuous discussions, media sharing, and cooperative undertakings on a worldwide scale.

At the core of WhatsApp's effect lies its capacity to encourage a significant feeling of interconnectedness, rising above geological, social, and etymological limits.

Vital to WhatsApp's part in cultivating worldwide interconnectedness is its accentuation on moment, continuous correspondence. The stage's informing usefulness permits clients to send instant messages, pictures, recordings, and voice notes flawlessly, empowering prompt trades independent of geological distances. This quickness has reformed the manner in which individuals associate, separating the obstructions of reality that once compelled correspondence.

The gathering visit include on WhatsApp intensifies its effect on interconnectedness by working with correspondence among various people at the same time. Companions, relatives, or partners dispersed across the globe can participate in bunch discussions, share refreshes, and work together on projects continuously. This component reinforces existing associations as well as makes virtual spaces where networks can shape and flourish, rising above the limits of actual nearness.

Besides, WhatsApp's voice and video call highlights contribute fundamentally to cultivating a feeling of interconnectedness. Past text-based correspondence, the capacity to hear a friend or family member's voice or see their face progressively adds a layer of closeness to communications. Video calls, specifically, overcome any issues between actual distances, permitting people to share minutes, festivities, and day to day existence as though they were in a similar room. This visual and hear-able association upgrades the nature of connections, making a significant feeling of presence notwithstanding the miles that different people.

WhatsApp's effect on interconnectedness stretches out to the domain of business and expert joint effort. The stage's adaptability considers the development of business gatherings, empowering groups to arrange, examine undertakings, and settle on choices continuously. This degree of network is priceless in a globalized economy where organizations work across various time regions and topographical areas. WhatsApp turns into a virtual office, cultivating a cooperative climate that rises above conventional working environment limits.

The stage's commitment to worldwide interconnectedness is likewise obvious in its job as a device for social trade and variety festivity. WhatsApp fills in as a stage for people to share parts of their social personality, whether through language, customs, or customs. Pictures and recordings displaying far-reaching developments, celebrations, or day to day existence permit clients to acquire experiences into the rich woven artwork of worldwide variety. Along these lines, WhatsApp turns into a scaffold, cultivating understanding and appreciation for the heap societies that exist together in the interconnected world.

Multilingualism is a sign of WhatsApp's worldwide reach. The stage upholds north of 60 dialects, permitting clients to impart in their favored language. This multilingual capacity is a vital part of encouraging interconnectedness, as it obliges the semantic variety that portrays our globalized society. Clients can flawlessly switch between dialects, separating language hindrances and advancing inclusivity in correspondence.

WhatsApp's effect on interconnectedness is additionally expanded by its openness. The stage works on cell phones, an innovation that has become progressively boundless worldwide. This openness guarantees that people from various financial foundations and districts can take part in the computerized discussion, adding to a more comprehensive interconnectedness that traverses across different socioeconomics.

The stage's obligation to client security and start to finish encryption upgrades its job as a confided in space for worldwide correspondence. Clients have a solid sense of safety sharing individual minutes, considerations, and data, it are safeguarded to know that their discussions. This trust is central to the advancement of significant associations in the computerized domain, adding to the feeling of interconnectedness that characterizes WhatsApp's effect.

WhatsApp has likewise assumed a urgent part in emergency correspondence and compassionate endeavors, exhibiting encouraging a feeling of worldwide solidarity potential. During catastrophic events, pandemics, or different crises, people and associations utilize the stage to spread data, coordinate aid projects, and offer help to impacted networks. This continuous correspondence adds to a worldwide consciousness of shared difficulties, cultivating an aggregate reaction that rises above public lines.

With regards to schooling, WhatsApp has turned into an essential instrument for working with learning and information trade on a worldwide scale. The stage's gathering visit highlight permits teachers and understudies to participate in conversations, share assets, and team up on projects regardless of their actual areas. This computerized study hall rises above conventional limits, establishing a globalized gaining climate where people from various regions of the planet add to an aggregate pool of information.

While WhatsApp's effect on interconnectedness is unquestionably significant, it isn't without difficulties and contemplations. The stage's omnipresence raises worries about the possible spread of deception and the requirement for computerized proficiency. In the interconnected universe of WhatsApp, data can circle quickly, contacting a huge crowd. Tending to falsehood requires a cooperative exertion, including innovation organizations, policymakers, and clients in advancing capable use and basic data utilization.

Security concerns likewise pose a potential threat in the computerized scene. While start to finish encryption defends the substance of messages, the metadata produced by client communications brings up issues about observation and information possession.

Finding some kind of harmony among protection and security is a continuous test that requires straightforward arrangements and progressing discourse between innovation suppliers and clients.

Besides, the computerized partition stays a critical obstacle in completely understanding the capability of WhatsApp's job in encouraging worldwide interconnectedness. Abberations in admittance to cell phones and the web ruin the stage's arrive at in specific locales and socioeconomics. Connecting this separation requires coordinated endeavors to upgrade computerized framework, further develop availability, and address financial imbalances.

WhatsApp's job in encouraging worldwide interconnectedness is additionally entwined with more extensive discussions about the effect of innovation on cultural standards and relational connections. The stage's effect on the elements of correspondence, the obscuring of individual and expert limits, and the development of accepted practices in the advanced age bring up issues about the drawn out results of this interconnectedness.

All in all, WhatsApp's effect on encouraging a feeling of worldwide interconnectedness is a demonstration of the groundbreaking force of computerized correspondence. The stage's constant informing, sight and sound abilities, and openness have reimagined the way people, networks, and organizations interface across borders. From individual connections and social trade to proficient coordinated effort and emergency correspondence, WhatsApp fills in as a virtual scaffold, uniting individuals in a common computerized space. As we explore the potential open doors and difficulties of this interconnected world, it is basic to move toward innovation use with mindfulness, obligation, and a guarantee to building a more comprehensive and associated worldwide local area.

In a time portrayed by globalization and interconnectedness, the idea of separating borders stretches out a long ways past the actual limits that different countries. Separating borders envelops a complex way to deal with destroying boundaries that obstruct progress, understanding, and participation on a worldwide scale. From international and monetary contemplations to social, innovative, and natural perspectives, separating borders includes a coordinated work to encourage joint effort, inclusivity, and a common feeling of obligation for the prosperity of the planet and its occupants.

At the international level, separating borders includes reconsidering customary ideas of sway and elevating strategic answers for clashes. The time of secluded country states is step by step giving way to a more interconnected reality where transnational issues, for example, environmental change, pandemics, and digital dangers, require cooperative and helpful reactions. Separating borders in this setting includes manufacturing peaceful accords, reinforcing discretionary ties, and cultivating a feeling of worldwide citizenship that rises above restricted public interests.

Financial boundaries, frequently appeared through exchange hindrances and protectionist arrangements, are basic parts of the separating borders story. Worldwide financial reconciliation can possibly lift millions out of neediness, prod development, and set out open doors for shared thriving. In any case, accomplishing this vision requires resolving issues like exchange awkward nature, financial disparity, and guaranteeing that the advantages of globalization are fairly appropriated. Separating monetary lines requires a promise to fair exchange rehearses, the expulsion of unreasonable duties, and the making of a comprehensive worldwide financial framework that helps all countries.

Socially, separating borders includes perceiving and commending the rich variety of human experience. In this present reality where correspondence and data stream across borders at a phenomenal rate, the chance to draw in with and value various societies has never been more prominent. Embracing social variety cultivates common figuring out, regard, and compassion, adding to a more amicable worldwide local area. Schooling, travel, and social trade programs make light of essential jobs in breaking social lines, empowering people to rise above generalizations and biases.

Mechanical progressions, especially in the domain of correspondence and data innovation, play made light of a vital part in breaking borders. The web, online entertainment, and computerized correspondence stages have made a virtual space where people from various corners of the world can interface, work together, and share thoughts progressively. The democratization of data through advanced stages has engaged people to get to information, express their voices, and partake in worldwide discussions. In any case, it likewise brings difficulties connected with falsehood, advanced isolates, and the moral utilization of innovation that should be tended to during the time spent separating mechanical lines.

Ecological worries, for example, environmental change and asset exhaustion, highlight the interconnectedness of the world and the desperation of breaking down borders for the aggregate prosperity of the planet. Ecological issues know no international limits, and their effect is felt worldwide. Tending to environmental change, safeguarding biodiversity, and guaranteeing reasonable asset the executives require global joint effort and a common obligation to natural stewardship. Breaking down borders in the natural setting includes rising above public interests to by and large address the difficulties that undermine the strength of the planet.

Chasing after separating borders, recognizing the job of schooling in molding the points of view and mentalities of individuals is fundamental. Schooling is an amazing asset for destroying generalizations, cultivating decisive reasoning, and imparting a feeling of worldwide citizenship. Educational plans that stress intercultural grasping, ecological stewardship, and the significance of joint effort add to making an age of people who are prepared to explore a world without counterfeit lines.

Separating borders isn't without its difficulties, and protection from this idea frequently comes from worries connected with loss of social character, financial disparity, and public safety. It is significant to address these worries through comprehensive strategies, open discourse, and a guarantee to tracking down arrangements that benefit all partners. A decent methodology that regards the extraordinary personalities of countries while perceiving the common difficulties that require aggregate activity is fundamental for the progress of breaking down borders.

The job of global associations and coalitions couldn't possibly be more significant in that frame of mind down borders account. Associations like the Unified Countries, the World Exchange Association, and local partnerships like the European Association assume vital parts in cultivating participation, intervening struggles, and laying out systems for tending to worldwide difficulties. Reinforcing these foundations and guaranteeing their adequacy is fundamental for the proceeded with progress in breaking down borders.

In the domain of medical care, separating borders is especially applicable, as proven by the worldwide reaction to pandemics like Coronavirus. The fast spread of irresistible illnesses rises above public boundaries, requiring an organized and cooperative work to contain and moderate the effect. Drives, for example, antibody dissemination, data sharing, and cooperative examination highlight the significance of worldwide fortitude in tending to wellbeing emergencies. Separating borders in medical care includes building strong and comprehensive wellbeing frameworks that can answer successfully to worldwide difficulties.

The strengthening of people and networks is a focal topic in the separating borders story. Enabled people are better prepared to add to their networks, participate in valuable exchange, and partake in the worldwide talk. Admittance to instruction, medical services, and financial open doors is essential to strengthening, and endeavors to separate lines ought to focus on drives that elevate underestimated networks and address foundational imbalances.

All in all, separating borders is an all encompassing and multi-layered idea that stretches out past the actual limits between countries. It includes tending to international, financial, social, innovative, and ecological boundaries to encourage an additional interconnected and cooperative world. Accomplishing this vision requires strategic endeavors, financial changes, social trade, mechanical development, and an aggregate obligation to tending to shared difficulties. Training, global associations, and the strengthening of people make light of essential jobs in the breaking borders story. As the world keeps on developing, embracing the ethos of separating borders isn't simply a decision however a need for making a reasonable, comprehensive, and amicable worldwide local area.

Chapter 4

Multimedia Messaging and Visual Culture

In the unique scene of contemporary correspondence, the combination of mixed media informing and visual culture has turned into a principal quality of how people put themselves out there, interface with others, and explore the computerized domain. Stages like WhatsApp, with its broad help for sight and sound informing, assume a significant part in molding this visual culture. The convergence of text, pictures, recordings, and other mixed media components rises above customary correspondence limits, leading to a rich embroidery of articulation that mirrors the different and interconnected nature of our globalized world.

The appearance of cell phones and high velocity web availability has changed the manner in which individuals impart, moving past the restrictions of message based messages. WhatsApp, with its easy to understand interface and boundless reception, has arisen as a vital participant in this sight and sound correspondence scene. The stage's help for pictures, recordings, voice messages, and archives permits clients to convey feelings, share encounters, and put themselves out there in manners that stretch out a long ways past the limitations of composed message.

Visual correspondence, worked with by media informing, has turned into a predominant method of articulation in the computerized age. Emoticons, GIFs, and stickers have become indispensable parts of contemporary discussions, giving a nuanced and expressive layer to message based correspondence. The visual language that has developed inside these stages fills in as a widespread code, rising above etymological and social obstructions, encouraging a common visual culture that associates people on a worldwide scale.

Pictures, as a type of visual correspondence, hold an extraordinary ability to convey complex feelings, recount stories, and catch minutes in time. The simplicity with which clients can share pictures on WhatsApp has changed the manner in which individuals archive and offer their lives. From individual achievements to worldwide occasions, pictures act as a general language that navigates geological and social limits, adding to the production of an aggregate visual story.

The stage's help for video informing adds one more aspect to interactive media correspondence. Clients can share pieces of their lives, participate in virtual narrating, or convey complex subtleties that go past what is conceivable with text alone. Video messages become a customized type of correspondence, permitting people to share words, yet additionally the tone, articulations, and subtleties of their messages. This visual narrating cultivates a more profound feeling of association and understanding in reality as we know it where actual distances can be immense.

Voice messages, one more aspect of WhatsApp's media capacities, carry a hearable aspect to computerized correspondence. The expressed word, with its sounds, accents, and feelings, adds a layer of legitimacy that text alone may battle to convey. Voice messages act as an extension between the quickness of spoken correspondence and the comfort of message, offering clients an adaptable and dynamic method of articulation.

WhatsApp's part in molding visual culture stretches out to its help for report sharing. Clients can flawlessly trade PDFs, Word records, and other document designs inside the stage. This usefulness is especially huge in proficient and cooperative settings, where the trading of records is vital to navigation, project coordination, and data sharing. The combination of record sharing inside an informing stage obscures the lines among correspondence and cooperation, changing the manner in which people and groups cooperate.

The convergence of interactive media informing and visual culture isn't without its difficulties and contemplations. The simplicity with which pictures and recordings can be shared raises worries about the spread of deception, counterfeit news, and unseemly substance. WhatsApp, in the same way as other different stages, wrestles with the need to offset client opportunity with mindful substance control. Finding some kind of harmony requires ceaseless endeavors to improve calculations, client revealing instruments, and coordinated effort with truth really taking a look at associations.

Besides, the fast development of visual culture on informing stages prompts conversations about the effect on customary composed language. The predominance of emoticons, stickers, and GIFs in advanced correspondence has prompted banters about whether this visual language is displacing or supplementing customary etymological articulation. Understanding the nuanced implications behind visual components becomes significant in a correspondence scene where pictures and images convey complex feelings and thoughts.

While mixed media informing on stages like WhatsApp adds to the democratization of visual articulation, it additionally brings up issues about protection and observation. The sharing of individual pictures, recordings, and voice messages inside computerized spaces achieves forward worries information security and the expected abuse of individual substance. Start to finish encryption, an element supported by WhatsApp, addresses a portion of these worries by guaranteeing that main the expected beneficiaries can get to the substance of messages.

The effect of media informing on visual culture reaches out past individual connections to the domain of showcasing, marking, and narrating. Organizations influence the visual capacities of stages like WhatsApp to make drawing in satisfied, share item refreshes, and associate with their crowd on a more private level. The instantaneousness of mixed media informing permits brands to lay out an immediate and legitimate association with shoppers, encouraging a feeling of straightforwardness and trust.

With regards to social developments and activism, interactive media informing turns into an integral asset for bringing issues to light and preparing networks. Pictures, recordings, and voice messages spread through stages like WhatsApp play had a critical impact in reporting social treacheries, enhancing underestimated voices, and exciting aggregate activity. The visual idea of these messages gets profound reactions, driving home the direness and significance of social causes.

Instruction, as well, has been significantly impacted by the combination of interactive media informing into the learning climate. Teachers use stages like WhatsApp to share sight and sound assets, connect with understudies in virtual conversations, and give visual clarifications of mind boggling ideas. The stage's gathering talk usefulness changes it into a virtual homeroom where understudies from various topographical areas can team up and learn together, rising above customary instructive limits.

As we explore the developing scene of mixed media informing and visual culture, it is fundamental to perceive the extraordinary capability of these advancements while staying aware of their effect on cultural standards and individual prosperity. The universality of visual components in advanced correspondence highlights the significance of media proficiency and the capacity to basically draw in with the visual substance that immerses our computerized spaces.

WhatsApp's part in molding visual culture isn't static; it develops with mechanical headways and client ways of behaving. The stage's obligation to protection, security, and dependable substance balance mirrors an acknowledgment of the moral contemplations that go with the help of interactive media informing. As innovation keeps on propelling, stages like WhatsApp will assume a focal part in characterizing the forms of visual culture, correspondence standards, and the manners by which people communicate their thoughts in the interconnected universe of the computerized age.

Taking everything into account, sight and sound informing and visual culture, as worked with by stages like WhatsApp, have become basic parts of contemporary correspondence. The intermingling of text, pictures, recordings, and other visual components changes the manner in which people put themselves out there, associate with others, and explore the computerized scene. From individual cooperations and narrating to business correspondence and social activism, media informing shapes a powerful visual culture that mirrors the different and interconnected nature of our globalized world. As we draw in with these advancements, it is fundamental to explore their intricacies with mindfulness, obligation, and a comprehension of their significant effect on the manners in which we impart and communicate our personalities in the computerized age.

4.1 Introduction of multimedia features in WhatsApp

The development of computerized correspondence has been set apart by a determined quest for more extravagant and more expressive types of cooperation. In this steadily evolving scene, the presentation of sight and sound elements in informing stages has arisen as a groundbreaking peculiarity. Among these stages, WhatsApp, with its far reaching client base and worldwide impact, plays had a significant influence in reshaping how people share and convey utilizing a different scope of media.

The coming of media informing on WhatsApp denoted a takeoff from the time of text-driven correspondence. Sent off in 2009, WhatsApp at first centered around message informing, furnishing clients with a basic and proficient method for sending messages to contacts across the globe. Notwithstanding, as innovation progressed and client assumptions advanced, the stage perceived the need to consolidate interactive media components to enhance the correspondence experience.

One of the critical achievements in this development was the presentation of picture partaking in 2012. This element permitted clients to send and get pictures inside their talks, changing discussions into visual encounters. The capacity to share photographs carried another aspect to correspondence, empowering clients to convey feelings, share encounters, and add an individual touch to their communications.

The mix of picture sharing likewise had significant ramifications for individual and social correspondence. Clients could now share minutes from their lives in a more clear and prompt manner. Birthday events, get-aways, festivities - these minutes could be caught and in a flash common with loved ones, rising above the restrictions of text based portrayals. The visual idea of pictures added a layer of lavishness to discussions, cultivating a more profound association among clients.

Expanding on the progress of picture sharing, WhatsApp extended its sight and sound abilities with the presentation of video partaking in 2013. This element permitted clients to share recordings straightforwardly inside the stage, further improving the extent of visual correspondence. Whether it was catching a short lived second or sharing a more drawn out story, the capacity to send recordings added flexibility to how clients articulated their thoughts.

The fuse of sight and sound highlights in WhatsApp was not just about growing the sorts of media that could be shared yet additionally about upgrading the UI. The stage went through overhauls to consistently oblige interactive media components. UIs were enhanced to guarantee a smooth encounter while connecting with pictures and recordings, making the mix of interactive media a necessary piece of the client venture.

Voice informing, presented in 2013, addressed one more element of media correspondence on WhatsApp. Clients could now send recorded voice messages, adding a more private and expressive component to their discussions. This component took care of the requirement for quick, unconstrained correspondence, permitting clients to pass tone and feeling on through their voices.

The meaning of these media highlights stretched out past private correspondence to incorporate business and expert communications. The capacity to share pictures, recordings, and voice messages became significant devices for organizations, empowering them to associate with their crowd in additional drawing in ways. From item dispatches to client assistance, interactive media correspondence on WhatsApp turned into a vital piece of the business tool compartment.

Moreover, WhatsApp perceived the significance of constant correspondence and presented the voice call highlight in 2015. This obvious a critical shift from text and mixed media informing to live, voice-to-voice discussions inside the stage. The presentation of voice calls extended the correspondence prospects as well as situated WhatsApp as an exhaustive specialized device, rivaling conventional voice calling administrations.

As the sight and sound capacities of WhatsApp kept on developing, the stage presented the video call highlight in 2016. Presently, clients could participate in up close and personal discussions, bringing a considerably more prominent feeling of quickness and closeness to their communications. Video calls turned into a fundamental device for special interactions, empowering clients to overcome any barrier of actual distances and associate in a more vivid way.

The development of media highlights on WhatsApp was tied in with improving correspondence as well as about tending to the different requirements of a worldwide client base. Perceiving the etymological variety across its client local area, WhatsApp acquainted the text-with discourse highlight in 2016. This permitted clients to change over instant messages into voice messages, improving availability and guaranteeing that language distinctions didn't upset correspondence.

In 2018, WhatsApp moved forward with the presentation of the Stickers highlight. Stickers, a type of visual articulation past customary emoticons, permitted clients to convey feelings, responses, and opinions in a more unique and connecting way. The sticker library developed over the long haul, including a large number of subjects and articulations, adding to the production of an exceptional visual language inside the stage.

WhatsApp Web, sent off in 2015, broadened the range of media informing past cell phones. Clients could now get to and send interactive media content from their work areas, working with a consistent change between gadgets. This element improved the accommodation of involving WhatsApp as well as extended the opportunities for sight and sound correspondence in proficient and cooperative settings.

The joining of media highlights in WhatsApp mirrors a more extensive pattern in computerized correspondence, where clients look for additional vivid and expressive ways of associating. The stage's obligation to client experience is clear in the persistent refinement and extension of its mixed media abilities. Embracing a client driven approach, WhatsApp has reliably adjusted to the developing necessities and inclinations of its different client base.

The presentation of sight and sound highlights in WhatsApp has not been without difficulties and contemplations. The stage has needed to explore issues connected with information security, content balance, and the dependable utilization of sight and sound components. The spread of falsehood, unseemly substance, and protection concerns provoked WhatsApp to execute measures, for example, start to finish encryption to safeguard client information and guarantee a solid correspondence climate.

Besides, the omnipresence of sight and sound correspondence brings up issues about the likely effect on composed language. The pervasiveness of pictures, recordings, and voice messages difficulties customary thoughts of message as the essential method of advanced correspondence. The developing visual language inside informing stages prompts conversations about the eventual fate of phonetic articulation in the computerized age.

As interactive media informing keeps on molding the manner in which people impart on WhatsApp, the stage stays at the very front of development. The combination of elements like vanishing messages in 2020 adds one more layer of dynamism to mixed media correspondence, permitting clients to send messages that evaporate after a set period. This component lines up with the advancing inclinations for vaporous, time-bound correspondence.

The effect of mixed media informing on visual culture stretches out past individual connections to impact cultural standards, social articulations, and, surprisingly, the domains of craftsmanship and inventiveness. Specialists, powerhouses, and content makers influence the visual and hear-able abilities of sight and sound stages to reach and draw in with worldwide crowds. WhatsApp, as a vital participant in this scene, adds to the democratization of visual articulation.

All in all, the presentation of media highlights in WhatsApp has been a groundbreaking excursion that reflects the more extensive development of computerized correspondence. From the beginning of message driven informing to the fuse of pictures, recordings, voice messages, and imaginative elements, WhatsApp has re-imagined how people communicate their thoughts in the advanced domain. The stage's obligation to client experience, security, and flexibility highlights its job as a key member in molding the fate of media correspondence. As clients keep on looking for additional expressive and vivid ways of interfacing, WhatsApp's excursion in sight and sound informing is a demonstration of the continuous development and development in the realm of computerized correspondence.

4.2 Cultural shift towards visual communication

The social scene of correspondence has gone through a significant change lately, set apart by a huge shift towards visual correspondence. This shift is portrayed by the rising predominance of pictures, recordings, emoticons, and other visual components in advanced associations. In this period of fast mechanical progression, stages like virtual entertainment, informing applications, and media sharing administrations have become basic to the manner in which people articulate their thoughts, associate with others, and explore the advanced domain. This social shift towards visual correspondence reflects changes in innovation as well as more profound cultural patterns, adjusting the actual texture of how we convey and share data.

The pervasiveness of cell phones, fast web, and the openness of media sharing stages play had an essential impact in driving the social shift towards visual correspondence. These mechanical headways have democratized the creation and utilization of visual substance, permitting people from different foundations to partake in the visual discussion. The ascent of stages like Instagram, Snapchat, and TikTok epitomizes this pattern, where clients participate in visual narrating, share snapshots of their lives, and convey through pictures and recordings.

One of the critical drivers of visual correspondence is the straightforwardness with which pictures and recordings can be made, shared, and consumed. The cameras implanted in cell phones have become progressively modern, empowering clients to catch top notch pictures and recordings no sweat. This democratization of visual creation enables people to share their viewpoints, encounters, and imagination, adding to a rich and various visual embroidery in the computerized space.

The ascent of visual correspondence is additionally intently attached to the constraints of customary text-based correspondence. Language, with its subtleties, social varieties, and potential for error, can in some cases miss the mark in conveying the profundity and intricacy of human articulation. Visual components, then again, rise above phonetic boundaries, offering a widespread language that can be perceived and appreciated across societies. The visual medium considers a more quick and instinctive association, evoking feelings and passing on messages in manners that words alone may battle to accomplish.

Emoticons and stickers, a type of visual shorthand, have become fundamental to the social shift towards visual correspondence. These little, expressive symbols convey feelings, responses, and opinions in a compact and generally grasped way. The utilization of emoticons has become so inescapable that they are presently a fundamental piece of computerized discussions, adding layers of subtlety and energy to message based messages. The broad reception of emoticons mirrors a longing for more extravagant, more emotive types of correspondence in the computerized age.

The pervasiveness of visual correspondence isn't restricted to individual cooperations; it has pervaded proficient and business correspondence too. Organizations influence visual components in their showcasing techniques, perceiving the force of pictures and recordings in catching consideration and passing on brand messages. Virtual entertainment stages, with their accentuation on visual substance, give organizations an immediate and connecting method for interfacing with their crowd, encouraging brand faithfulness and acknowledgment.

Visual stages like Pinterest, which spins around the curation and sharing of pictures, represent the social shift towards outwardly determined associations. Clients on Pinterest make advanced sheets to gather and share pictures that resound with their inclinations, yearnings, and way of life. This stage is a demonstration of the human tendency towards visual articulation, where people build their characters and convey parts of their characters through organized visual substance.

The appearance of increased reality (AR) and augmented reality (VR) advances further speeds up the social shift towards visual correspondence. AR overlays advanced data onto the actual world, improving the manner in which people cooperate with their environmental factors. Snapchat channels, for instance, use AR to expand clients' countenances with fun loving movements and impacts, changing the demonstration of taking a selfie into an outwardly innovative and engaging experience. Essentially, VR stages give vivid conditions where clients can convey, work together, and share encounters in manners that go past conventional message or video-based cooperations.

Virtual entertainment stages play had a significant impact in molding and enhancing the social shift towards visual correspondence. Instagram, with its emphasis on photograph and video sharing, has turned into a visual-driven stage that impacts how people curate and offer their lives.

The Tales highlight on stages like Instagram and Snapchat permits clients to share fleeting minutes through a succession of pictures and recordings, making a story that lines up with the transient idea of contemporary computerized correspondence.

The ascent of TikTok, a stage based on short-structure recordings, typifies the social shift towards outwardly determined content. TikTok's organization urges clients to make and share imaginative, frequently comical recordings, encouraging a worldwide local area of content makers and buyers. The stage's calculation, which designers content suggestions in light of client inclinations, has added to the virality of patterns and difficulties, making a dynamic and outwardly captivating biological system.

The social shift towards visual correspondence isn't without its difficulties and contemplations. The straightforwardness with which visual substance can be made and dispersed raises worries about the spread of deception, the effect on emotional wellness, and issues connected with protection and assent. The visual idea of stages likewise presents difficulties for content balance, as calculations and human arbitrators wrestle with the intricacies of directing pictures and recordings at scale.

Besides, the social shift towards visual correspondence prompts conversations about the possible effect on education and the composed word. As visual components become the overwhelming focus in computerized cooperations, there are worries about a possible decrease in customary proficiency abilities, with some contending that the power of visual correspondence might prompt a deficiency of subtlety, profundity, and decisive reasoning that composed language can give.

The convergence of visual correspondence with social and cultural standards is apparent in the domain of computerized activism and social developments. Visual substance assumes an essential part in recording and dispersing data about friendly treacheries, preparing networks, and bringing issues to light about significant causes. Stages like Instagram, where pictures are imparted to strong subtitles and hashtags, act as integral assets for enhancing voices and pushing for social change.

The shift towards visual correspondence additionally has suggestions for training, where instructors influence sight and sound components to improve the opportunity for growth. Instructive substance makers utilize visual narrating, recordings, and intuitive illustrations to make sense of perplexing ideas, making learning seriously captivating and available. Stages like YouTube have become centers for instructive substance, democratizing admittance to information and taking care of different learning styles.

All in all, the social shift towards visual correspondence is a multi-layered peculiarity that mirrors the unique exchange between innovation, cultural patterns, and human articulation. Stages like web-based entertainment, informing applications, and media sharing administrations have become channels for this shift, giving people amazing assets to put themselves out there outwardly, associate with others, and partake in a worldwide visual culture. As visual correspondence keeps on developing with innovative headways, cultural standards, and client ways of behaving, it is crucial for approach these progressions with a nuanced comprehension of their effect on human communication, social articulation, and the manner in which we explore the undeniably visual scene of the computerized age.

4.3 Influence of WhatsApp on contemporary visual language

The impact of WhatsApp on contemporary visual language is a convincing investigation into the manners by which this informing stage has reshaped the elements of correspondence. WhatsApp, with its worldwide client base surpassing two billion, has turned into an indispensable piece of everyday cooperations, and its effect on visual correspondence is significant. As a stage that at first centered around text-based informing, WhatsApp's development into a media rich specialized instrument has reflected changing mechanical capacities as well as essentially impacted the more extensive social scene, forming the visual language of our interconnected world.

WhatsApp's excursion into visual correspondence can be followed through its essential consolidation of sight and sound elements. The stage's presentation of picture partaking in 2012 denoted a vital second, permitting clients to send and get pictures inside their visits. This basic yet strong expansion changed discussions, giving a visual setting to messages and making a more vivid correspondence experience. The joining of pictures permitted clients to share minutes, feelings, and articulations such that outperformed the limitations of composed text.

The resulting consideration of video partaking in 2013 further extended WhatsApp's visual language. Clients could now send brief video cuts, encouraging a more extravagant and more powerful type of correspondence. The capacity to convey development, articulations, and stories through recordings added profundity to communications, adding to the advancement of a visual vernacular inside the stage. Video sharing turned into a method for sharing encounters, recounting stories, and interfacing in a more nuanced way.

Voice informing, presented in 2013, addressed one more aspect of WhatsApp's introduction to mixed media correspondence. While not outwardly arranged, voice messages added a hear-able layer to discussions, permitting clients to convey tone, feelings, and setting through their voices. This expansion exhibited WhatsApp's obligation to different types of articulation, recognizing the multi-tactile nature of human correspondence.

The mix of emoticons and stickers further hardened WhatsApp's effect on contemporary visual language. Emoticons, at first presented in 2015, immediately turned into a basic piece of advanced correspondence. These little, expressive images permitted clients to convey feelings, responses, and opinions in a brief and generally figured out way. The resulting expansion of stickers in 2018 gave clients a greater library of outwardly powerful articulations, adding to the stage's visual language variety.

WhatsApp's hug of visual components was tied in with adding highlights as well as about improving UIs to consistently oblige media. The client experience was custom-made to guarantee that drawing in with pictures, recordings, and other visual substance was just about as natural as text-based informing. This comprehensive way to deal with configuration assumed a pivotal part in molding the client's impression of WhatsApp as a stage that consistently coordinates visual and literary correspondence.

The effect of WhatsApp on contemporary visual language reaches out past individual cooperations to impact more extensive social and cultural standards. The stage's broad reception has added to the standardization of visual correspondence, with clients consolidating pictures, recordings, and emoticons into their everyday discussions. This social shift is especially obvious in more youthful ages, where visual components are many times fundamental to how they articulate their thoughts and draw in with others.

WhatsApp's job in forming visual language is unpredictably connected to its effect on social articulations and character. Clients influence visual components to convey parts of their characters, share social subtleties, and express innovativeness. The stage turns into a material for self-portrayal, where people curate their visual presence through profile pictures, notices, and the sight and sound they decide to share. This interchange of visuals and character adds to the development of a computerized visual culture inside the WhatsApp people group.

The stage's effect on contemporary visual language is additionally obvious in the domain of individual connections and associations. WhatsApp fills in as a virtual space where people keep up with and reinforce connections through visual components. Whether it's sharing photographs of day to day existence, sending loving emoticons, or taking part in energetic sticker trades, the visual language of WhatsApp turns into a common code that upgrades the nature of relational associations.

The impact of WhatsApp on visual language stretches out to expert and business correspondence. In a globalized computerized scene, organizations influence the stage's media capacities to associate with clients, share item updates, and cultivate brand commitment. Visual substance, like pictures and recordings, turns into an integral asset for promoting and narrating, permitting organizations to make an additional customized and outwardly convincing story.

The stage's effect on business correspondence is additionally underscored by the presentation of WhatsApp Business, a specific variant custom-made for little and medium-sized undertakings. This emphasis of WhatsApp empowers organizations to communicate with clients in a more organized way, using visuals for item features, client care, and advancements. The joining of business functionalities inside the stage highlights the flexibility of WhatsApp's visual language in different settings.

WhatsApp's effect on contemporary visual language is especially noticeable with regards to social developments and activism. Visual substance, whether it's pictures, recordings, or visual images, turns into an intense instrument for bringing issues to light, preparing networks, and enhancing voices. The stage's inescapable reach permits activists and promotion gatherings to share visuals that report social treacheries, pass on strong messages, and flash discussions that rise above geological limits.

In the instructive scene, WhatsApp's effect on visual language is apparent in the manner teachers and understudies influence media components for learning. Instructive substance makers utilize the stage to share visual clarifications, recordings, and pictures that supplement conventional educating techniques. WhatsApp bunches become virtual homerooms, cultivating cooperative learning conditions where understudies draw in with visual substance to upgrade how they might interpret complex ideas.

The reconciliation of mixed media highlights in WhatsApp has not been without difficulties and contemplations. The simplicity with which visual substance can be shared raises worries about the spread of deception, counterfeit news, and unseemly substance. WhatsApp has carried out measures, for example, start to finish encryption and content balance to address these difficulties, stressing its obligation to keeping a protected and capable correspondence climate.

Protection concerns likewise come to the very front in the domain of visual correspondence. The sharing of individual pictures, recordings, and sight and sound substance inside computerized spaces brings up issues about information security and the possible abuse of individual substance. WhatsApp's devotion to start to finish encryption plans to address these worries, guaranteeing that clients have command over who can get to their visual correspondences.

As WhatsApp proceeds to develop and present new highlights, its effect on contemporary visual language is probably going to extend. The presentation of highlights like vanishing messages in 2020 mirrors a guarantee to furnishing clients with dynamic and vaporous approaches to drawing in with visual substance. This component lines up with the advancing inclinations for time-bound correspondence and adds to the ease of visual language inside the stage.

All in all, WhatsApp's impact on contemporary visual language is a complex investigation into how this informing stage has re-imagined the elements of correspondence. From the beginning of text-driven informing to the reconciliation of pictures, recordings, emoticons, and stickers, WhatsApp plays had a critical impact in molding a different and dynamic visual language. The stage's effect reaches out past individual associations to impact cultural standards, social articulations, business correspondence, and even activism. As clients proceed to embrace and adjust to the visual language of WhatsApp, it turns into a microcosm of the more extensive social shift towards visual correspondence in the interconnected universe of the computerized age.

In contemporary society, media informing has turned into a fundamental piece of correspondence, essentially molding the manner in which people articulate their thoughts and cooperate with the world. The combination of text, pictures, recordings, and other visual components in informing stages has altered correspondence, rising above the impediments of customary text-based trades. This shift towards mixed media informing has led to a visual culture that penetrates different parts of our lives, impacting how we impart, see data, and build our personalities.

The coming of cell phones and the expansion of high velocity web play played significant parts in the boundless reception of sight and sound informing. Stages like WhatsApp, Snapchat, Instagram, and Facebook Courier have become essential mechanisms for relational correspondence, permitting clients to consistently share a blend of message, photographs, recordings, and emoticons. The promptness and extravagance of these sight and sound messages empower people to pass on feelings, encounters, and stories in a more nuanced and drawing in way.

Visual components in mixed media informing offer a strong method for self-articulation and narrating. Emojis and emoticons, for example, have developed into an all inclusive language, rising above phonetic boundaries to convey feelings and responses. The utilization of GIFs (Designs Exchange Configuration) adds one more layer of expressiveness, permitting clients to convey humor, fervor, or mockery with a powerful visual component. The incorporation of these visual parts changes messages from simple transports of data to intelligent and sincerely thunderous trades.

Past private correspondence, media informing has saturated proficient and open arenas, modifying the elements of how data is spread and consumed. Virtual entertainment stages act as useful assets for people and associations to impart visual substance to a worldwide crowd. From news updates to promoting efforts, the reconciliation of media components improves the effect and commitment of the message. This shift towards visual correspondence has provoked organizations and people the same to focus on the formation of outwardly engaging substance to catch and hold crowd consideration.

The ascent of visual culture in media informing has likewise prompted a change in the utilization of information and data. Stages like Snapchat and Instagram spearheaded the vaporous idea of visual substance, with stories that vanish after a set period. This organization has impacted different stages, prompting a more transient and outwardly determined way to deal with data utilization. The curtness of these visual stories takes special care of the contemporary inclination for fast and absorbable substance, testing customary long-structure news coverage.

In addition, the impact of mixed media informing on visual culture stretches out to the development and projection of individual personalities. Web-based entertainment stages, specifically, have become virtual materials for people to arrange and introduce their lives through pictures and recordings. The painstakingly created feel of Instagram takes care of and Snapchat stories add to the development of online personas, obscuring the lines between the computerized and actual domains. The visual parts of media informing offer an organized look into the existences of people, impacting how they are seen by their internet based networks.

Be that as it may, the unavoidable idea of visual culture in media informing likewise raises concerns with respect to security, genuineness, and the effect on mental prosperity. The steady sharing of organized pictures and recordings might make ridiculous assumptions and add to a culture of correlation, possibly prompting insecurities and nervousness. The mission for the ideal visual portrayal via web-based entertainment can bring about a twisted reality, testing the validness of online cooperations.

Besides, the far and wide utilization of media informing raises protection worries as people share close minutes, individual encounters, and touchy data through visual mediums. The potential for abuse or accidental sharing of private substance features the requirement for powerful protection settings and client mindfulness. Finding some kind of harmony among sharing and safeguarding individual data becomes vital in exploring the intricacies of media informing in the computerized age.

As visual culture keeps on advancing in mixed media informing, the job of man-made consciousness (artificial intelligence) and expanded reality (AR) turns out to be progressively unmistakable. Simulated intelligence fueled highlights, like facial acknowledgment, picture examination, and computerized channels, upgrade the client experience by giving customized and intuitive components. The coordination of AR into informing applications permits clients to overlay virtual components onto their true climate, adding a layer of imagination and inundation to correspondence.

While the headways in sight and sound informing offer energizing prospects, they likewise raise moral contemplations. The utilization of computer based intelligence in picture control and deepfakes presents difficulties in knowing credible visual substance from controlled or manufactured material.

As media informing turns out to be more complex, tending to the moral ramifications of artificial intelligence driven highlights becomes basic to keep up with trust and respectability in advanced correspondence.

All in all, media informing has introduced a visual culture that saturates our own, proficient, and open arenas. The combination of text, pictures, recordings, and intelligent components has changed correspondence into a dynamic and expressive experience. The impact of visual culture reaches out past private trades, molding how data is scattered, consumed, and how private personalities are developed on the web.

While the ascent of visual culture in media informing offers remarkable open doors for self-articulation and correspondence, it likewise presents difficulties connected with protection, credibility, and moral contemplations. Exploring these difficulties requires a smart methodology that adjusts the advantages of visual correspondence with the obligations of guaranteeing protection, genuineness, and moral principles. As mixed media informing keeps on developing, its effect on visual culture will without a doubt shape the eventual fate of correspondence in significant ways, impacting how people associate, offer, and experience their general surroundings.

Chapter 5

WhatsApp in Business Communication

In the consistently developing scene of correspondence, the combination of innovation plays had a critical impact in reshaping how organizations connect with their partners. One outstanding progression in this domain is the joining of WhatsApp into business correspondence techniques. Initially planned as an individual informing stage, WhatsApp's far and wide reception provoked organizations to investigate its true capacity as an expert instrument.

The universality of cell phones and the worldwide prominence of WhatsApp have made it an appealing mechanism for organizations looking for proficient and prompt correspondence channels. WhatsApp Business, a committed stage for ventures, arose as a reaction to this interest. Its highlights are custom-made to meet the extraordinary requirements of organizations, cultivating a consistent association among organizations and their clients.

One of the vital benefits of involving WhatsApp in business correspondence is its openness. With more than two billion month to month dynamic clients, WhatsApp gives a gigantic client base that organizations can take advantage of. The application's easy to understand interface guarantees that the two clients and workers can undoubtedly explore its elements, working with speedy and successful correspondence.

The continuous idea of WhatsApp is one more component that has added to its prevalence in the business world. Dissimilar to customary methods of correspondence, for example, email, WhatsApp empowers texting, taking into consideration quick trades of data. This continuous ability demonstrates priceless in situations where convenient correspondence is basic, for example, tending to client questions, planning group projects, or giving quick updates.

WhatsApp Business presents a few elements explicitly intended for hierarchical use. Mechanized informing is one such component that empowers organizations to set up predefined reactions to normal questions. This smoothes out client service as well as guarantees consistency in correspondence. Moreover, the capacity to make a business profile with fundamental data, for example, contact subtleties, business hours, and a concise portrayal improves the expert picture of an organization on the stage.

The utilization of WhatsApp in business correspondence stretches out past client associations. Interior correspondence inside an organization is similarly urgent, and WhatsApp has demonstrated to be a powerful device in such manner. Representative gatherings can be made to work with group cooperation, empowering individuals to share updates, archives, and other applicable data flawlessly. The mixed media abilities of the stage further upgrade the correspondence experience, permitting clients to share pictures, recordings, and reports inside the application.

As organizations progressively embrace remote work plans, the requirement for productive virtual specialized devices turns out to be more articulated. WhatsApp, with its versatile first methodology, adjusts well to the advancing elements of remote work. The capacity to lead voice and video calls straightforwardly from the application upgrades the flexibility of WhatsApp as a far reaching correspondence stage.

Moreover, WhatsApp's start to finish encryption guarantees a protected climate for delicate business correspondences. This encryption highlight has been a vital figure imparting trust among clients, especially in situations where protection and information security are principal concerns. Organizations can use this solid stage for secret conversations, talks, and the trading of exclusive data.

The joining of WhatsApp into the more extensive range of business activities isn't restricted to correspondence alone. The stage's business Programming interface (Application Programming Point of interaction) opens up opportunities for mechanization and mix with other business instruments.

This Programming interface permits organizations to incorporate WhatsApp into their current CRM (Client Relationship The executives) frameworks, giving a consistent progression of information between stages. Computerization of specific correspondence cycles can fundamentally improve productivity, opening up HR for additional perplexing undertakings.

Showcasing is another region where WhatsApp has made huge advances. The stage's transmission records and gathering highlights empower organizations to all the while contact a huge crowd. This direct and designated way to deal with promoting has demonstrated successful, particularly in enterprises where customized correspondence is vital. Moreover, the notice include permits organizations to share constant updates, advancements, and declarations with their crowd.

Be that as it may, the incorporation of WhatsApp into business correspondence isn't without challenges. One prominent concern is the potential for data overburden. The consistent stream of messages, warnings, and updates can be overpowering, prompting diminished efficiency and expanded feelings of anxiety among representatives. Organizations need to lay out clear rules on the fitting utilization of WhatsApp to moderate these difficulties and work out some kind of harmony among correspondence and efficiency.

Additionally, the casual idea of informing on WhatsApp can some of the time obscure the lines among individual and expert correspondence. This casual tone, while reasonable for specific settings, may not be suitable for all business connections. Organizations should lay out correspondence conventions to keep an expert picture while involving WhatsApp as a business device.

The worldwide idea of business implies that organizations frequently draw in with clients and accomplices from assorted social foundations. While WhatsApp offers a multilingual connection point, organizations should be aware of social subtleties in their correspondence. Error of messages because of social contrasts can prompt false impressions and possibly hurt business connections.

Regardless of these difficulties, the advantages of involving WhatsApp in business correspondence are significant. The stage's broad reception, continuous capacities, and secure correspondence highlights make it a significant resource for organizations hoping to improve their correspondence systems. As organizations keep on adjusting to the advanced time, integrating WhatsApp into their specialized tool stash can add to further developed client relations, smoothed out interior cycles, and in general authoritative productivity.

Looking forward, the eventual fate of WhatsApp in business correspondence holds energizing prospects. As innovation keeps on progressing, new elements and functionalities might arise, further growing the capacities of WhatsApp as a business instrument. Joining with arising advancements, for example, man-made brainpower and expanded reality could open up inventive ways for organizations to interface with their crowds.

All in all, WhatsApp has developed from an individual informing application to a flexible and key instrument for organizations. Its broad fame, continuous capacities, and secure correspondence highlights pursue it a favored decision for both inner and outside correspondence. As organizations explore the intricacies of the cutting edge computerized scene, WhatsApp stands apart as a dependable and viable stage, adding to improved network and cooperation in the expert domain.

5.1 The integration of WhatsApp in business strategies

The combination of WhatsApp into business techniques has become progressively pervasive lately, denoting a change in the manner in which organizations speak with both inner groups and outside partners. WhatsApp, initially planned as an individual informing application, has changed into a multi-layered device that offers one of a kind advantages for organizations across different businesses. This coordination is driven by the stage's far and wide worldwide use, ongoing correspondence capacities, and a scope of elements customized for proficient use.

One of the key variables adding to the mix of WhatsApp into business systems is its unmatched reach. With north of two billion month to month dynamic clients, WhatsApp gives a gigantic client base that ranges across landmasses. This omnipresence guarantees that organizations can use the stage to interface with a different crowd, from clients and clients to workers and accomplices. The application's accessibility on both Android and iOS gadgets further expands its openness, making it a flexible instrument for organizations, everything being equal.

The continuous idea of WhatsApp has shown to be a unique advantage in the domain of business correspondence. Dissimilar to customary correspondence channels that include delays, for example, email, WhatsApp works with texting. This promptness is especially significant in circumstances where ideal correspondence is basic, for example, tending to client requests, planning project timetables, or answering arising business open doors. The proficiency acquired through continuous correspondence can contribute fundamentally to an organization's general efficiency.

WhatsApp Business, a devoted stage for ventures, acquaints includes explicitly planned with improve proficient correspondence. One such element is the business profile, permitting organizations to make an extensive profile with fundamental data, including contact subtleties, business hours, and a short portrayal. This not just gives an expert picture to the business yet in addition fills in as a helpful reference point for clients looking for data.

Computerization is one more key part of WhatsApp Business that lines up with current business systems. Robotized reactions to regularly posed inquiries smooth out client assistance and commitment. Organizations can set up predefined reactions, decreasing the requirement for manual mediation in routine connections. This recoveries time as well as guarantees consistency in correspondence, adding to a better client experience.

Interior correspondence is a foundation of compelling business tasks, and WhatsApp has arisen as an important device for cultivating joint effort inside associations. The making of representative gatherings empowers groups to convey flawlessly, share refreshes, and team up on projects. The interactive media abilities of WhatsApp further improve inward correspondence by permitting the sharing of pictures, recordings, and reports straightforwardly inside the application.

As the worldwide business scene goes through a change with a rising accentuation on remote work, WhatsApp's versatile first methodology adjusts well to the requirements of current endeavors. The stage's voice and video assembling highlights work with virtual conferences and conversations, decreasing the dependence on conventional specialized strategies. This is particularly appropriate in situations where up close and personal associations are not attainable, advancing productivity and adaptability in the cutting edge work environment.

Security and protection concerns are principal in the business world, and WhatsApp resolves these issues through its start to finish encryption. This security include guarantees that messages and calls are scrambled and must be gotten to by the planned beneficiaries. For organizations participated in touchy correspondences, for example, dealings or the trading of restrictive data, this degree of safety is pivotal in building and keeping up with trust.

The mix of WhatsApp into business procedures isn't restricted to correspondence alone; it stretches out to computerization and joining with other business devices. WhatsApp's Business Programming interface gives an entryway to organizations to incorporate the stage into their current frameworks, like CRM (Client Relationship The board) devices. This incorporation smoothes out processes, considering a consistent progression of information and correspondence between various stages.

Showcasing is a region where WhatsApp has made huge advances, offering organizations an immediate and customized channel to contact their crowd. The transmission records and gathering highlights empower organizations to all the while send designated messages to an enormous crowd. The notice include considers the sharing of ongoing updates, advancements, and declarations, upgrading the showcasing capacities of the stage.

Notwithstanding the heap benefits, the coordination of WhatsApp into business systems accompanies its arrangement of difficulties. One prominent concern is the potential for data over-burden. The consistent stream of messages, warnings, and updates can overpower clients, prompting diminished efficiency and expanded feelings of anxiety. Laying out clear rules on the suitable utilization of WhatsApp is urgent to moderate these difficulties and find some kind of harmony among correspondence and efficiency.

The casual idea of informing on WhatsApp is one more thought for organizations. While the stage's easygoing tone might be reasonable for specific settings, keeping an expert picture is fundamental in numerous business collaborations.

Organizations should lay out correspondence conventions to guarantee that the utilization of WhatsApp lines up with the expert norms anticipated in the business climate.

Social contemplations add one more layer of intricacy to the joining of WhatsApp into business methodologies. In a globalized business scene, organizations cooperate with clients and accomplices from different social foundations. While WhatsApp offers a multilingual connection point, organizations should be aware of social subtleties in their correspondence to stay away from misconceptions that might actually hurt business connections.

Looking forward, the eventual fate of WhatsApp in business techniques holds promising potential outcomes. As innovation keeps on progressing, new elements and functionalities might arise, further growing the capacities of WhatsApp as a business instrument. Mix with arising advancements, for example, man-made brainpower and increased reality could open up creative ways for organizations to interface with their crowds and smooth out their activities.

All in all, the combination of WhatsApp into business systems mirrors a change in perspective in the manner organizations approach correspondence. The stage's worldwide reach, continuous capacities, and exhibit of business-explicit elements position it as a significant device for endeavors looking to upgrade their correspondence methodologies. As organizations explore the intricacies of the computerized period, WhatsApp stands apart as a solid and compelling stage, adding to further developed client relations, smoothed out inner cycles, and in general hierarchical effectiveness.

5.2 WhatsApp Business features and their impact

The approach of WhatsApp Business has presented a horde of highlights customized to meet the novel requirements of undertakings, impacting the manner in which organizations draw in with clients, smooth out inside correspondence, and improve in general functional effectiveness. These highlights, planned with an emphasis on impressive skill and usefulness, fundamentally affect different parts of business tasks.

One of the champion elements of WhatsApp Business is the Business Profile. This element permits organizations to make a committed profile that incorporates fundamental data, for example, contact subtleties, business hours, area, and a concise portrayal. This fills in as a virtual retail facade for organizations on the stage, furnishing clients with fast admittance to significant data. The effect of the Business Profile is two-overlay: it upgrades the expert picture of the business and works with consistent correspondence by introducing crucial subtleties in a succinct and effectively open configuration.

Mechanization is a vital part of WhatsApp Business, and the Robotized Reactions highlight is a demonstration of this concentration. Organizations can set up predefined reactions to normal questions, computerizing the underlying phases of client communication. This smoothes out client care as well as guarantees consistency in reactions.

The effect of Computerized Reactions is especially articulated in situations where organizations get a high volume of habitually clarified pressing issues. Via mechanizing these reactions, organizations can assign HR to additional perplexing inquiries, working on generally speaking proficiency.

The Names highlight in WhatsApp Business gives an organized way to organizations to sort out and classify their connections. Organizations can appoint marks to talks in view of various models, for example, the phase of the deals pipe, the idea of the question, or the client's status. This element is important for organizations managing an enormous volume of client requests, as it empowers them to successfully focus on and deal with their collaborations more. The effect of Marks is clear in the upgraded association and smoothed out administration of client correspondence.

Another component that has had an extraordinary effect is the Business Programming interface (Application Programming Connection point). The Programming interface permits organizations to incorporate WhatsApp into their current frameworks, like CRM (Client Relationship The executives) instruments. This coordination works with a consistent progression of information between various stages, disposing of the requirement for manual information passage and diminishing the probability of mistakes. The effect of the Business Programming interface reaches out past correspondence; it adds to by and large handle streamlining and upgrades the proficiency of business activities.

WhatsApp Business Gatherings assume a vital part in encouraging inward correspondence inside associations. Worker gatherings can be made to work with group joint effort, empowering individuals to share updates, records, and other significant data in a unified space. The effect of WhatsApp Business Gatherings is especially huge with regards to remote work, where virtual joint effort is fundamental. The media abilities of the stage further advance inward correspondence by permitting the sharing of pictures, recordings, and archives straightforwardly inside the application.

The ongoing correspondence abilities of WhatsApp Business are exemplified by its Voice and Video Calling highlights. These elements empower organizations to lead virtual gatherings, meetings, and conversations straightforwardly inside the application. The effect of this constant correspondence is especially imperative in situations where up close and personal communications are not attainable, for example, during remote work or while managing global clients. The capacity to settle on voice and video decisions improves the flexibility of WhatsApp Business as a far reaching specialized instrument.

The Security and Protection highlights of WhatsApp Business, including start to finish encryption, address basic worries in the business climate. The start to finish encryption guarantees that messages and calls are secure and must be gotten to by the expected beneficiaries.

For organizations participated in delicate correspondences, for example, talks or the trading of restrictive data, this degree of safety is principal in building and keeping up with trust. The effect of these security highlights stretches out past individual collaborations, adding to the general believability of WhatsApp Business as a solid correspondence stage.

Promoting on WhatsApp Business is worked with through highlights, for example, Broadcast Records and Gathering Informing. The Transmission Records highlight permits organizations to send designated messages to different contacts at the same time, making an immediate and customized channel for correspondence. Bunch Informing empowers organizations to make networks and draw in with their crowd in a cooperative climate. The effect of these showcasing highlights is apparent in the immediate and prompt association they give among organizations and their clients, encouraging commitment and brand dependability.

The Notice highlight in WhatsApp Business fills in as a unique stage for sharing continuous updates, advancements, and declarations. This element permits organizations to feature their items or administrations imaginatively and gives an extra road to client commitment. The effect of Notices in showcasing lies in their capacity to pass on data in an outwardly engaging organization, catching the consideration of clients and building up brand perceivability.

Nonetheless, the reconciliation of WhatsApp Business includes additionally presents difficulties that organizations need to explore. The casual idea of informing on the stage may in some cases obscure the lines among individual and expert correspondence. Finding some kind of harmony and laying out clear correspondence conventions are pivotal to keeping an expert picture while involving WhatsApp Business as a device. Also, the potential for data over-burden, given the consistent stream of messages and notices, expects organizations to carry out rules that focus on correspondence without compromising efficiency.

Social contemplations likewise become possibly the most important factor while using WhatsApp Business highlights, particularly in a globalized business climate. Organizations interfacing with clients and accomplices from assorted social foundations should be aware of social subtleties to guarantee compelling correspondence and stay away from mistaken assumptions. Adjusting correspondence techniques to line up with social assumptions is fundamental for organizations trying to areas of strength for assemble aware connections.

Looking forward, the future effect of WhatsApp Business highlights holds guarantee as innovation keeps on developing. The joining of arising advances, like man-made brainpower and increased reality, could additionally upgrade the capacities of WhatsApp Business. The potential for further developed mechanization, customized client encounters, and creative promoting techniques opens up new roads for organizations to investigate.

Taking everything into account, the effect of WhatsApp Business highlights on business correspondence and tasks is complex. From improving impressive skill through Business Profiles to smoothing out client service with Robotized Reactions, each element adds to the stage's flexibility as a thorough business specialized device.

As organizations keep on utilizing these highlights, they should explore difficulties, adjust correspondence methodologies to social settings, and stay cautious to arising patterns that could shape the future effect of WhatsApp Business in the advancing scene of business correspondence.

5.3 Shaping cultural expectations in customer engagement

Molding social assumptions in client commitment has arisen as a basic part of contemporary business methodologies. As organizations work in an undeniably globalized world, the variety of their client base requires a nuanced approach that considers social contrasts, inclinations, and assumptions. Client commitment, incorporating collaborations and connections among organizations and their clients, is a powerful interaction impacted by social standards, values, and correspondence styles.

Understanding the social setting is key to molding client commitment procedures. Culture incorporates a great many components, including language, customs, customs, normal practices, and values. By digging into these viewpoints, organizations can tailor their client commitment ways to deal with reverberate with assorted crowds. Social skill, the capacity to explore and adjust to various social settings, is significant for organizations trying to construct significant and deferential associations with clients across the globe.

Language is a foundation of social correspondence, and organizations should be sensitive to the phonetic subtleties that impact client commitment. This goes past simple interpretation; it includes understanding the social undertones and nuances of language use. For instance, certain words or expressions that are harmless in one culture might convey various implications or suggestions in another. Consequently, organizations should put resources into language restriction to guarantee that their informing isn't just precisely deciphered yet in addition socially significant and delicate.

Social subtleties reach out to non-verbal correspondence also. Signals, non-verbal communication, and looks can convey implications that might vary across societies. What is viewed as a positive motion in one culture might be deciphered diversely in another. Organizations drawing in with clients from different social foundations should be aware of these non-verbal signs to keep away from false impressions and guarantee that their correspondence is deferential and generally welcomed.

Social qualities assume a huge part in forming client assumptions. Various societies might focus on different qualities like independence, community, progressive system, or populism. Understanding these social qualities assists organizations adjust their client commitment techniques to the assumptions for their interest group. For example, in societies that esteem independence, customized and custom-made client encounters might be more valued, while in collectivist societies, bunch situated approaches might be more viable.

Normal practices direct satisfactory conduct inside a given culture, and organizations should explore these standards to encourage positive client commitment. This incorporates understanding how social progressive systems work, the job of orientation in correspondence, and the propriety of specific subjects or approaches. Sticking to normal practices constructs trust and compatibility with clients, as it exhibits regard for their social setting and a guarantee to figuring out their interesting requirements.

In forming social assumptions in client commitment, organizations should perceive the meaning of time direction. Various societies put shifting accentuation on the past, present, or future. For instance, societies with a past-situated center might esteem custom and history, while those with a future-situated point of view might focus on development and progress. Adjusting client commitment techniques to the time direction of the objective culture upgrades the importance and reverberation of the business' contributions.

Innovation plays had a significant impact in forming social assumptions in client commitment. The worldwide interconnectedness worked with by computerized stages has made an assumption for consistent and quick correspondence. Clients, no matter what their social foundation, presently expect quick reactions to requests, customized communications, and the accommodation of advanced exchanges. Organizations that influence innovation to live up to these assumptions gain an upper hand in the present speedy and interconnected business scene.

Online entertainment stages have become instrumental in forming social assumptions in client commitment. These stages act as channels for organizations to cooperate with clients on a worldwide scale. Be that as it may, social awareness is foremost in online entertainment commitment. What might be OK happy or correspondence style in one culture might be seen contrastingly in another. Organizations need to tailor their web-based entertainment presence to line up with the social assumptions for their assorted crowd, cultivating inclusivity and pertinence.

In the domain of client care, the joining of man-made reasoning (simulated intelligence) has changed the scene. Chatbots and remote helpers, controlled by man-made intelligence, give quick reactions to client questions, adding to the assumption for moment delight in client commitment. While computer based intelligence driven client service can upgrade effectiveness, organizations should guarantee that these advances are socially mindful and fit for exploring the subtleties of assorted client connections.

Social assumptions in client commitment likewise reach out to moral contemplations. Various societies might have shifting assumptions about business morals, corporate social obligation, and supportability. Organizations that adjust their practices to the moral assumptions for their clients show a pledge to social and ecological qualities, building trust and steadfastness.

Moral contemplations are especially striking in the present globalized commercial center, where clients frequently look for arrangement with organizations that share their qualities.

Personalization is a critical component in forming social assumptions in client commitment. Clients currently expect customized encounters that resound with their singular inclinations and social foundation. This expects organizations to gather and investigate information on client ways of behaving, inclinations, and social pointers. By utilizing information examination, organizations can tailor their contributions, showcasing techniques, and correspondence to line up with the particular assumptions for different client sections.

Social variety inside organizations likewise assumes a vital part in forming social assumptions in client commitment. Having a different labor force empowers organizations to draw on a scope of points of view, experiences, and social skills. This variety improves inner imagination and advancement as well as positions the business to more readily comprehend and meet the different requirements of its client base. Organizations that focus on variety and consideration are better prepared to explore the intricacies of social assumptions in client commitment.

In the accommodation and the travel industry, social assumptions are especially articulated. Explorers from various social foundations bring interesting inclinations, assumptions, and responsive qualities. Organizations in this industry should be proficient at multifaceted correspondence, offering encounters that take special care of different preferences while regarding social standards. From language contemplations to culinary inclinations, understanding and adjusting to social assumptions are fundamental for progress in the worldwide the travel industry market.

The effect of social assumptions on client commitment is apparent in the domain of web based business. Online retailers taking special care of a worldwide crowd should consider social elements in web composition, UI, installment choices, and client support. Adjusting internet business stages to line up with the social assumptions for different clients improves the general client experience and adds to the progress of online organizations on a worldwide scale.

In spite of the developing acknowledgment of the significance of social assumptions in client commitment, organizations some of the time face difficulties in carrying out compelling procedures. One normal test is the intricacy of exploring different social scenes. With clients from various districts, each with its remarkable social subtleties, organizations might find it trying to foster a one-size-fits-all methodology. Fitting techniques to explicit locales or social sections requires a nuanced comprehension of each social setting.

Also, the unique idea of social assumptions represents a continuous test for organizations. Societies develop over the long run, affected by outside elements like globalization, mechanical headways, and social patterns.

Organizations should stay coordinated and receptive to these changes, constantly rethinking their client commitment methodologies to line up with developing social assumptions. This versatility is urgent for keeping up with pertinence and seriousness in a quickly changing business climate.

All in all, molding social assumptions in client commitment is a complex undertaking that requires a profound comprehension of social subtleties, values, and correspondence styles. Organizations that focus on social capability and designer their client commitment techniques to line up with different social assumptions gain an upper hand in the worldwide commercial center. From language limitation to innovation driven arrangements, organizations should explore the complexities of social variety to fabricate significant and enduring associations with their clients. As the business scene keeps on developing, the capacity to shape social assumptions in client commitment will stay a urgent calculate the outcome of ventures across enterprises.

Chapter 6

Privacy and Encrypted Communication

Protection and scrambled correspondence have become central focuses in contemporary conversations encompassing innovation, information, and individual security. As the advanced scene develops, the requirement for secure and confidential correspondence has developed dramatically. This shift is driven by a rising consciousness of the worth of individual information, worries about reconnaissance, and an acknowledgment of the potential weaknesses inborn in the interconnected world. This paper investigates the ideas of protection and scrambled correspondence, their importance, and the advancing scene where they work.

Protection, with regards to correspondence, alludes to one side of people to control their own data and the degree to which they decide to share it. This key basic freedom is cherished in different global shows and lawful structures. Protection isn't just about keeping specific parts of one's life stowed away yet additionally about having command over who approaches individual data and the way things are utilized. In the computerized age, where data is a product, protecting security has turned into a perplexing test.

Encoded correspondence is a mechanical reaction to the basic of protection in the computerized domain. Encryption includes the utilization of calculations to change over data into a coded design, making it indistinguishable without the fitting decoding key. This cycle guarantees that regardless of whether caught, the correspondence stays secure and private. Encoded correspondence is applied across different stages, including informing applications, email administrations, and online exchanges. The objective is to make a safe channel through which data can be traded without the gamble of unapproved access.

The coming of scrambled correspondence applications denoted a critical change in the manner people and organizations moved toward protection in the computerized space. WhatsApp, Sign, Wire, and other informing stages acquainted end-with end encryption, a vigorous type of encryption where just the shipper and the expected beneficiary can translate the message. This degree of safety gives a feeling of confirmation to clients, cultivating trust in the protection of their computerized discussions.

The meaning of security in correspondence stretches out past private messages to envelop delicate data, for example, monetary exchanges, medical care records, and legitimate interchanges. For organizations, guaranteeing the security of client information, exclusive data, and inner correspondences is vital. The outcomes of a security break can be extreme, prompting monetary misfortunes, reputational harm, and lawful implications. In this manner, the reconciliation of scrambled specialized devices has turned into an essential basic for associations planning to safeguard delicate data.

One of the vital benefits of scrambled correspondence is its part in countering reconnaissance and unapproved access. In a period where information is an important ware, worries about mass reconnaissance by states, partnerships, and malignant entertainers have escalated. Encoded correspondence goes about as a defend against ridiculous interruption, furnishing clients with a degree of insurance against unapproved admittance to their own and delicate information.

The discussion around security and encoded correspondence acquired conspicuousness in the outcome of disclosures by informants like Edward Snowden, who uncovered the degree of worldwide reconnaissance directed by knowledge organizations. These disclosures highlighted the weakness of computerized correspondence to mass observation and the requirement for strong security measures. Accordingly, there was a flood in the turn of events and reception of encoded specialized devices that focused on client protection and security.

Nonetheless, the boundless utilization of encoded correspondence affects public safety. Policing contend that the utilization of start to finish encryption ruins their capacity to screen and forestall crimes. The strain between protection supporters and those upholding for outstanding admittance to scrambled interchanges mirrors a more extensive cultural discussion about tracking down the right harmony among security and security.

Lately, the idea of protection has gone through a change with the ascent of web-based entertainment stages, online administrations, and the assortment of tremendous measures of client information. The plans of action of numerous tech organizations are based on the adaptation of client information through designated publicizing. This has prompted worries about the disintegration of security, as people are progressively followed, profiled, and designated in view of their web-based conduct. The commodification of individual information has brought up moral issues about the obligation of tech organizations to safeguard client protection.

In the midst of these worries, security guidelines like the European Association's Overall Information Assurance Guideline (GDPR) and the California Purchaser Protection Act (CCPA) have been authorized to enable people with more noteworthy command over their own information. These guidelines stress straightforwardness, assent, and the option to be neglected, mirroring a worldwide work to lay out a structure that shields individual security privileges in the computerized age.

The reception of protection driven advancements, including encoded specialized apparatuses, lines up with the standards implanted in security guidelines. Tech organizations are progressively perceiving the market interest for items and administrations that focus on client protection. Security highlights, for example, the capacity to erase messages, limit information maintenance, and control who can get to specific data, have become key differentiators in the cutthroat scene of advanced correspondence stages.

The ascent of security centered digital forms of money, like Monero and Zcash, further highlights the developing interest for protection in advanced exchanges. These digital currencies use progressed cryptographic methods to guarantee the secrecy of clients and the classification of their monetary exchanges. Security driven coins mirror a longing for monetary protection, repeating the more extensive cultural shift towards recovering command over private data.

While the reception of encoded correspondence is a positive step towards upgrading protection, it isn't without challenges. One prominent test is the likely abuse of scrambled stages for unlawful exercises. Criminal components, including psychological militant associations and cybercriminals, have been known to take advantage of encoded specialized devices to plan and facilitate criminal operations past the scope of policing. Finding some kind of harmony among protection and security stays a complex and developing test for policymakers and technologists.

The ascent of quantum processing represents one more test to the ongoing encryption norms. Quantum PCs can possibly break broadly utilized encryption calculations, delivering current safety efforts outdated. As the improvement of quantum-safe encryption calculations advances, the requirement for nonstop development in the field of online protection becomes apparent. Adjusting to arising dangers and remaining in front of potential weaknesses is a continuous basic in the domain of scrambled correspondence.

The job of huge tech organizations in molding the security scene is a basic part of the developing talk. The duopoly of Google and Apple, with their separate working frameworks (Android and iOS), gives them huge impact over the security highlights accessible to billions of clients. The two organizations have made security a focal topic in their new item refreshes, presenting highlights, for example, application following straightforwardness and upgraded protection controls. Notwithstanding, questions stay about the degree to which these protection drives are driven by a veritable obligation to client security or are roused by administrative tensions and market rivalry.

With regards to encoded correspondence, the discussion frequently revolves around the compromises between comfort, ease of use, and security. While start to finish encryption gives an elevated degree of safety, it can likewise present difficulties concerning key administration, client confirmation, and record recuperation. Finding some kind of harmony among security and client experience is a ceaseless course of refinement for designers and specialist co-ops.

The crossing point of protection and man-made consciousness (artificial intelligence) adds one more layer of intricacy to the discussion. Man-made intelligence calculations, filled by immense datasets, can possibly gather bits of knowledge into client conduct, inclinations, and even feelings. This raises worries about the degree to which man-made intelligence frameworks regard client security and whether the sending of computer based intelligence lines up with moral contemplations. The improvement of security protecting artificial intelligence advances becomes basic to address these worries and encourage trust in computer based intelligence driven applications.

The continuous development of security and scrambled correspondence meets with more extensive cultural conversations on computerized privileges, observation free enterprise, and the moral obligations of innovation organizations. As people become more aware of the worth of their own information, there is a developing interest for straightforwardness, responsibility, and moral practices in the tech business. The development towards decentralized innovations, blockchain-based arrangements, and client controlled information biological systems mirrors a craving to engage people with more noteworthy command over their computerized impression.

Teaching people about the significance of security and encoded correspondence is a pivotal part of encouraging a protection cognizant society. Numerous clients may not be completely mindful of the dangers related with unstable correspondence channels or the degree to which their own information is gathered and used. Security instruction drives expect to enable people with the information and devices expected to come to informed conclusions about their advanced connections.

6.1 WhatsApp's commitment to user privacy

WhatsApp's obligation to client protection has been a focal precept of its central goal since its commencement. As one of the world's most broadly utilized informing applications, WhatsApp has reliably underscored the significance of giving a safe and confidential correspondence stage for its clients. This responsibility is especially significant in a time where worries about computerized protection, information security, and observation have become central.

Start to finish encryption remains as the foundation of WhatsApp's obligation to client security. This exceptional safety effort guarantees that main the shipper and the expected beneficiary of a message can unscramble and peruse its items. Indeed, even WhatsApp itself can't get to the messages traded on its foundation because of this encryption.

This degree of protection insurance goes past the business standard, underscoring WhatsApp's devotion to establishing a correspondence climate where client discussions stay secret and secure.

The execution of start to finish encryption isn't restricted to instant messages however ever reaches out to voice calls, video calls, and interactive media content shared inside the application. This comprehensive way to deal with encryption highlights Whats-App's obligation to defending different types of correspondence traded by its clients. Whether people are sharing individual messages, delicate data, or media records, the start to finish encryption guarantees that their correspondence stays private and unavailable to unapproved substances.

WhatsApp's obligation to client security likewise remembers serious areas of strength for a for information maintenance. The stage doesn't store client messages on its servers whenever they are conveyed. This fleeting nature of message stockpiling improves client security by limiting the computerized impression of their correspondences. Clients can have certainty that their messages are not chronicled on WhatsApp servers, adding to a feeling of control and independence over their own information.

The straightforwardness of WhatsApp's protection rehearses is one more part of its obligation to client trust. The stage gives clients clear and available data about its security strategies and practices. This straightforwardness reaches out to the sort of information gathered, the way things are utilized, and the safety efforts set up. By keeping clients informed, WhatsApp enables them to settle on informed conclusions about their security and comprehend the actions taken to safeguard their information.

WhatsApp's obligation to client security is additionally shown through its reaction to legitimate solicitations for client information. The stage complies with a severe strategy of uncovering client data just because of substantial legitimate solicitations and inside the limits of pertinent regulations. WhatsApp's straightforwardness reports give bits of knowledge into the number and nature of government demands for client information, offering clients perceivability into the stage's connections with policing while at the same time maintaining security privileges.

The organization's obligation to client protection is supported by its status as a free substance inside the Facebook organization. While WhatsApp is essential for the more extensive Facebook biological system, it works with a different and committed security strategy. This partition stresses WhatsApp's particular obligation to client protection, guaranteeing clients that their information on the informing stage is treated with a degree of independence from different substances inside the Facebook group of organizations.

WhatsApp's devotion to client protection isn't static; it advances with the changing scene of innovation and security assumptions. In light of client criticism and arising security concerns, WhatsApp routinely refreshes its highlights and protection settings.

The stage integrates client driven protection highlights, for example, two-step check, which adds an additional layer of safety to client accounts. By consistently upgrading its protection tool stash, WhatsApp shows a proactive way to deal with tending to developing security challenges.

WhatsApp has likewise been a supporter for protection freedoms on a worldwide scale. The stage assumed a significant part in testing government commands that compromise client security, especially in the domain of encryption. WhatsApp has reliably guarded the option to give start to finish encryption as a principal security measure, opposing endeavors to debilitate this security in different locales. This support positions WhatsApp as a hero for client security inside its foundation as well as in more extensive cultural and lawful settings.

The obligation to client protection is obvious in WhatsApp's way to deal with promoting. Not at all like other informing stages that examine client messages to serve designated promotions, WhatsApp utilizes a remarkable model that focuses on client protection. WhatsApp doesn't utilize the substance of client messages for the purpose of promoting. This responsibility guarantees that the stage stays a specialized instrument instead of a vehicle for designated publicizing, protecting the security of client discussions.

WhatsApp's obligation to client protection isn't without difficulties and debates. The presentation of WhatsApp's refreshed protection strategy in 2021 ignited boundless conversations and concerns. The strategy changes, at first saw by certain clients as a compulsory sharing of information with Facebook, prompted a flood in client movement to elective informing stages. Because of the kickback, WhatsApp explained that the arrangement basically impacted associations with organizations and didn't think twice about security of individual messages.

This occurrence, while featuring the awareness of clients towards protection changes, additionally displayed WhatsApp's responsiveness to client concerns. The stage participated in proactive correspondence, explanations, and instructive drives to address confusions and reduce client misgivings. The episode highlighted the basic job of straightforwardness and clear correspondence in keeping up with client trust around security related matters.

WhatsApp's obligation to client security is likewise reflected in its endeavors to battle deception and safeguard client security. The stage utilizes encryption for protection as well as an action to forestall the spread of bogus data. By making it actually infeasible to get to the substance of messages, even WhatsApp can't check the exactness of data traded between clients. This obligation to security, in any case, presents difficulties with regards to fighting falsehood, featuring the sensitive harmony among protection and the requirement for data respectability.

The eventual fate of WhatsApp's obligation to client protection is probably going to include proceeded with advancements in security highlights, upgraded client training, and promotion for security privileges. As innovation advances and protection concerns develop, WhatsApp will probably adjust its systems to address new difficulties while remaining consistent with its center obligation to giving a safe and confidential correspondence stage.

The worldwide administrative scene around security is likewise expected to impact WhatsApp's methodology. The stage will probably keep on exploring complex administrative conditions, teaming up with policymakers and adjusting its practices to conform to developing protection norms. As protection turns into an undeniably focal worry for clients and controllers the same, WhatsApp's obligation to client protection positions it as a central member in molding the fate of private and secure computerized correspondence.

All in all, WhatsApp's obligation to client protection is woven into the texture of its personality and tasks. The execution of start to finish encryption, straightforward protection rehearses, freedom inside the Facebook organization, and proactive promotion for protection privileges on the whole highlight WhatsApp's commitment to making a safe and confidential correspondence space for its clients. While difficulties and discussions might emerge, WhatsApp's responsiveness and obligation to tending to client concerns further set its situation as a forerunner in focusing on and shielding client protection in the powerful scene of computerized correspondence stages.

6.2 Influence of end-to-end encryption on digital trust

The impact of start to finish encryption (E2EE) on computerized trust is a huge and complex part of the developing scene of online correspondence. Start to finish encryption, a strong safety effort that guarantees just the shipper and the expected beneficiary of a message can unscramble and peruse its items, has reshaped the elements of computerized trust in more ways than one. This paper investigates the effect of start to finish encryption on advanced trust, analyzing its job in cultivating client certainty, tending to protection concerns, and forming the more extensive discussion around security in the computerized age.

One of the essential manners by which start to finish encryption impacts computerized entrust is by giving clients an uplifted conviction that all is good and security. In conventional correspondence models, messages communicated over advanced networks are defenseless to capture attempt and observation. E2EE tends to this weakness by scrambling the substance of messages so that even the specialist co-op working with the correspondence can't get to the decoded information. This degree of security assurance imparts trust in clients that their computerized cooperations are safeguarded from unapproved access.

Computerized trust is firmly connected to clients' view of the security of their own data. The predominance of information breaks, cyberattacks, and examples of unapproved access has uplifted worries about the wellbeing of online correspondence. Start to finish encryption arises as an incredible asset in moderating these worries, guaranteeing clients that their messages, whether message, voice, or mixed media, stay classified and difficult to reach to outer substances. Subsequently, the reception of stages with E2EE has become inseparable from a promise to client protection and security.

The job of start to finish encryption in computerized trust is especially articulated with regards to informing applications. Stages like WhatsApp, Sign, and Wire have acquired conspicuousness for their execution of E2EE. Clients float towards these applications for their easy to understand interfaces as well as for the affirmation that their confidential discussions are protected from inquisitive eyes. The ubiquity of

E2EE-empowered informing applications highlights the interest for secure correspondence channels and the critical job encryption plays in building and keeping up with advanced trust.

For organizations and associations working in the advanced domain, the impact of start to finish encryption on computerized trust stretches out to the shielding of delicate data. Whether it is restrictive information, licensed innovation, or private interchanges, the execution of E2EE adds an additional layer of security against unapproved access. This degree of safety not just cultivates trust among clients, accomplices, and workers yet in addition adds to the general standing and believability of the business.

In the domain of computerized trust, straightforwardness is a key variable. Clients are progressively knowing about the protection practices of the stages they draw in with. Start to finish encryption adds to straightforwardness by plainly depicting the limits of information access. Since the unscrambling keys are held exclusively by the source and the beneficiary, even the stage working with the correspondence can't interpret the substance. This straightforwardness upgrades clients' certainty that their messages are not expose to reconnaissance or information mining, encouraging a feeling of command over their computerized communications.

The advanced trust caused by start to finish encryption isn't exclusively about safeguarding against outside dangers yet in addition tends to worries about interior weaknesses. With the rising consciousness of insider dangers and information breaks starting from inside associations, E2EE turns into a vital instrument for getting interior correspondences. Organizations that focus on the reception of scrambled specialized instruments exhibit a promise to defending delicate data from outside programmers as well as from possible inward dangers, supporting computerized trust among partners.

Start to finish encryption likewise assumes an essential part in computerized trust inside the setting of remote work and cooperation. As the worldwide labor force turns out to be progressively decentralized, the dependence on advanced specialized instruments for far off cooperation heightens. E2EE gives a solid channel to groups to trade delicate data, examine secret matters, and team up without the apprehension about unapproved access. Without any actual nearness, the affirmation of secure advanced correspondence becomes central to building trust among remote groups.

The effect of start to finish encryption on advanced trust is interwoven with the more extensive discussion on client independence and command over private information. The standards of information minimization and client agree are integral to numerous protection guidelines, and E2EE lines up with these standards by restricting the openness of client information. Stages that focus on start to finish encryption engage clients with more noteworthy command over their advanced impression, permitting them to convey and share data without unjustifiable reconnaissance or information abuse. This strengthening adds to a good criticism circle, where clients, feeling more in charge of their information, are bound to trust and draw in with stages that focus on their security.

Nonetheless, the impact of start to finish encryption on computerized trust isn't without its intricacies and contemplations. One remarkable test emerges from the strain among protection and security objectives. While E2EE improves security by forestalling unapproved admittance to correspondence content, it likewise presents difficulties for policing trying to battle crimes. The harmony between security privileges and the requirement for public wellbeing is a fragile one, and the execution of E2EE frequently winds up at the focal point of discussions around legal admittance to encoded correspondences.

The strain among protection and security is exemplified in the continuous talk about the "going dim" issue. This term alludes to the difficulties looked by policing when they experience scrambled correspondences that they can't translate, even with lawful approval. Security advocates contend that the conservation of E2EE is fundamental to shield people from outlandish reconnaissance, while policing the requirement for components that permit legitimate admittance to scrambled correspondences in light of a legitimate concern for public wellbeing.

The potential for abuse of start to finish encryption by malevolent entertainers is one more thought in the computerized trust condition. While the actual innovation is a strong device for getting correspondence, it can likewise be utilized by people and gatherings participating in illegal exercises. The obscurity given by E2EE raises worries about its expected use for planning crimes, psychological militant plots, or other pernicious undertakings past the span of policing. Finding some kind of harmony that jam client protection while tending to genuine security concerns stays a mind boggling challenge.

The impact of start to finish encryption on advanced trust isn't uniform across all correspondence stages and administrations. While informing applications like WhatsApp and Signal focus on E2EE, different stages, particularly those determined by publicizing models, may adopt an alternate strategy. The plan of action of adapting client information for designated publicizing makes a strain among protection and benefit. Clients of stages that depend on information digging for publicizing might be more doubtful about the stage's obligation to computerized trust, given the intrinsic irreconcilable circumstance.

The effect of start to finish encryption on computerized trust additionally converges with the more extensive discussion about the moral obligations of innovation organizations. In a time where public attention to protection issues is uplifted, organizations that focus on client security and straightforward protection rehearses are bound to acquire and hold the trust of their client base. The reconciliation of E2EE, joined by clear correspondence about its execution and advantages, turns into an essential move for organizations trying to construct and keep up with computerized trust.

As the scene of advanced correspondence keeps on developing, the impact of start to finish encryption on computerized trust is probably going to escalate. Security guidelines like the Overall Information Assurance Guideline (GDPR) in Europe and the California Buyer Protection Act (CCPA) in the US highlight the worldwide shift towards enabling clients with more noteworthy command over their own information. Start to finish encryption lines up with the standards of these guidelines, situating itself as a central component in the journey for computerized trust.

The continuous improvement of security safeguarding innovations, remembering headways for cryptographic conventions and decentralized models, further expands the effect of start to finish encryption on computerized trust. Advancements that upgrade the security and protection of computerized correspondence without compromising client experience are probably going to shape the eventual fate of computerized trust. From zero-information verifications to homomorphic encryption, the field of protection saving advances holds guarantee for tending to current difficulties and pushing the limits of computerized trust in the years to come.

All in all, the impact of start to finish encryption on computerized trust is a nuanced and dynamic exchange between security, protection, and client independence. E2EE has arisen as an essential component in encouraging computerized entrust by furnishing clients with a solid and confidential channel for correspondence. Its effect reaches out past individual security to impact the more extensive discussion on information assurance, moral innovation rehearses, and the advancing connection among clients and computerized stages. As the advanced scene keeps on developing, the impact of start to finish encryption on computerized trust will stay fundamental to forming.

6.3 Broader societal implications of privacy concerns in the digital age

The more extensive cultural ramifications of protection worries in the computerized age are multi-layered, enveloping many issues that stretch out past individual encounters to shape the texture of contemporary social orders. As mechanical progressions keep on reclassifying the manners by which data is gathered, shared, and used, worries about security have turned into a focal topic in cultural talk. This article investigates the significant ramifications of security worries on different parts of society, including the disintegration of individual independence, the effect on vote based system, the job of reconnaissance, and the advancing connection among people and innovation.

Protection, when thought about an essential right, faces extraordinary difficulties in the computerized age. The pervasive assortment of individual information by innovation organizations, web-based entertainment stages, and different elements has prompted a steady disintegration of individual independence. People end up under steady reconnaissance, both unmistakable and secret, as their web-based exercises, inclinations, and ways of behaving are carefully followed and investigated. The subsequent loss of command over one's very own data decreases the capacity to arrive at independent conclusions about what parts of one's life are shared and with whom, generally adjusting the elements of individual organization.

The disintegration of individual independence because of protection concerns is especially articulated with regards to designated publicizing. The unavoidable following of people's web-based conduct permits organizations to make exceptionally definite profiles, empowering the conveyance of customized promotions. While designated promoting can improve the pertinence of showcasing messages, it comes at the expense of individual security. Clients frequently wind up exposed to a consistent flood of notices custom-made to their inclinations, obscuring the line between certifiable decision and manipulative impact. This peculiarity brings up moral issues as well as has more extensive cultural ramifications by molding purchaser conduct and inclinations in view of calculations as opposed to genuine individual organization.

Security concerns likewise cross with the popularity based texture of social orders. The coming of web-based entertainment as an essential wellspring of data and correspondence has brought up issues about the effect of algorithmic curation on open talk. The calculations utilized by web-based entertainment stages, driven by the craving to expand client commitment, frequently make channel air pockets and carefully protected areas, building up people's current convictions and restricting openness to different points of view. This particular openness can add to the polarization of society, ruining helpful discourse and compromising the central standards of a sound majority rule government.

Besides, the control of online data, filled by information driven focusing on and disinformation crusades, represents a huge danger to the respectability of popularity based processes. The capacity to miniature objective explicit socioeconomics with customized political messages can impact popular assessment and influence electing results. Protection concerns are interlaced with the more extensive test of guaranteeing the straightforwardness and decency of computerized spaces, underscoring the requirement for hearty guidelines and moral norms to defend the vote based goals of educated and unprejudiced public talk.

The expansion of observation advancements, both legislative and corporate, raises significant worries about individual security and common freedoms. Legislatures, driven by public safety objectives, progressively send observation apparatuses that reach from facial acknowledgment frameworks to mass information assortment programs. The omnipresent idea of observation innovations, combined with their true capacity for misuse, represents an immediate danger to residents' on the right track to security.

The reconnaissance state, frequently legitimized for the sake of public wellbeing, presents a sensitive harmony among security and individual opportunities, provoking a basic assessment of the cultural ramifications of unavoidable observation.

Corporate observation, driven by benefit thought processes, likewise assumes a urgent part in forming cultural elements. Innovation organizations accumulate huge measures of client information, which are then adapted through designated promoting and other plans of action. The commodification of individual data changes people into items, exchanged the commercial center of information driven free enterprise. The cultural ramifications of this reconnaissance driven economy incorporate the centralization of force among tech goliaths, the disintegration of security as a major right, and the potential for prejudicial practices in view of algorithmic profiling.

Notwithstanding legislative and corporate reconnaissance, the ascent of shared observation, worked with by the universality of cell phones and web-based entertainment, adds one more layer to the protection worries in the computerized age. People continually report and offer parts of their lives internet, adding to a culture of consistent perceivability. While this sharing can encourage associations and local area, it likewise obscures the limits among public and confidential circles. The strain to organize a web-based persona that lines up with cultural assumptions can bring about self-reconnaissance, where people eagerly give up parts of their protection in return for social approval.

The commodification of individual data and the disintegration of security have suggestions for minimized and weak populaces. Security concerns cross with issues of value, as specific segment gatherings might be excessively impacted by the unfortunate results of information driven rehearses. For instance, algorithmic predispositions in regions, for example, recruiting, loaning, and policing propagate existing social imbalances. Protection turns into a civil rights issue, with underestimated networks confronting elevated dangers of segregation and reconnaissance, enhancing existing inconsistencies.

The disintegration of protection additionally has mental ramifications for people and society at large. The steady consciousness of being under reconnaissance, combined with the strain to adjust to cultural standards in computerized spaces, can add to a feeling of nervousness and self-oversight. The apprehension about judgment and the longing for social approval might drive people to adjust to apparent assumptions, smothering innovativeness and genuine self-articulation. Thus, the cultural ramifications of protection concerns stretch out past the legitimate and administrative domains to influence the actual texture of individual and aggregate personality.

The appearance of savvy urban communities, portrayed by the coordination of advanced innovations into metropolitan foundation, raises extra protection concerns. The arrangement of sensors, reconnaissance cameras, and information examination in broad daylight spaces empowers urban areas to gather and dissect huge measures of data about occupants.

While these advances guarantee productivity gains and worked on metropolitan preparation, they likewise acquaint difficulties related with information security, assent, and the potential for ridiculous government interruption into people's lives. The cultural ramifications of brilliant urban communities highlight the requirement for mindful and moral ways to deal with metropolitan innovation arrangement.

The exchange between security concerns and psychological well-being is an arising area of cultural thought. The steady availability and openness in the advanced domain can add to sensations of detachment, correlation tension, and the strain to introduce an admired adaptation of one's life. Web-based entertainment, specifically, has been connected to psychological well-being issues, including gloom and tension. The observation culture, where people feel noticed and judged, can add to a feeling of weakness and effect in general prosperity. As cultural conversations around psychological wellness gain conspicuousness, the job of computerized security in encouraging a better web-based climate turns out to be progressively pertinent.

Endeavors to address protection worries in the computerized age include a mix of administrative structures, mechanical developments, and cultural mindfulness. Security guidelines, like the Overall Information Assurance Guideline (GDPR) in Europe and the California Customer Protection Act (CCPA) in the US, mean to enable people with more noteworthy command over their own information. These guidelines stress straightforwardness, assent, and the option to be neglected, mirroring a developing acknowledgment of the need to rebalance the unevenness of force among people and substances that gather and cycle their information.

Mechanical developments, including protection safeguarding innovations, for example, start to finish encryption and decentralized structures, assume a crucial part in relieving security concerns. These advances focus on client control and security, giving apparatuses to people to safeguard their computerized protection. Decentralized frameworks, based on standards of client strengthening and information possession, offer an option in contrast to the concentrated models that overwhelm the ongoing advanced scene. The turn of events and reception of such advancements add to a change in outlook in which protection isn't simply a right yet a plan standard implanted in the design of computerized frameworks.

Cultural mindfulness and schooling are essential parts of tending to protection worries in the advanced age. People should be educated about the ramifications regarding their internet based exercises, the worth of their own information, and the potential dangers related with information driven rehearses. Advancing computerized proficiency and protection schooling becomes basic to engage people to arrive at informed conclusions about their web based presence and to advocate for their security privileges.

The cultural ramifications of protection worries in the computerized age highlight the requirement for an all encompassing and cooperative methodology. State run administrations, innovation organizations, common society, and people all assume parts in molding the fate of computerized security.

Chapter 7

WhatsApp's Role in Information Dissemination

WhatsApp's job in data spread has become progressively conspicuous and powerful in the computerized age. As one of the most broadly utilized informing stages internationally, WhatsApp has changed the manner in which individuals convey and share data. This paper investigates the multi-layered parts of WhatsApp's job in data scattering, looking at its effect on private correspondence, the spread of information and data, the difficulties related with falsehood, and the advancing elements of social collaborations inside the stage.

At its center, WhatsApp is an informing application intended for secure and moment correspondence between people or gatherings. Its easy to understand interface, cross-stage similarity, and start to finish encryption have added to its broad reception. In the domain of individual correspondence, WhatsApp fills in as an essential channel for message informing, voice calls, and video calls, empowering clients to interface with companions, family, and partners across geological limits. The stage's part in working with immediate, private, and continuous correspondence has reclassified relational cooperations in the computerized age.

WhatsApp's effect on data spread reaches out past private correspondence to the domain of information and media sharing. The stage's highlights, for example, the capacity to send instant messages, pictures, recordings, and reports, make it a flexible instrument for sharing an extensive variety of data. Clients can rapidly disperse news stories, updates, and mixed media content to people or gatherings, encouraging a fast and productive progression of data. This element has added to the decentralization of information utilization, enabling clients to go about as the two shoppers and wholesalers of data inside their groups of friends.

The gathering visit highlight on WhatsApp enhances its part in data spread, empowering clients to make networks in view of shared interests, affiliations, or geographic vicinity. These gathering talks act as microcosms of data biological systems, where members effectively share and examine news, occasions, and subjects of common interest. This distributed data trade inside shut bunches recognizes WhatsApp from other virtual entertainment stages, making customized and contextualized spaces for data sharing.

While WhatsApp's job in data dispersal brings benefits, it additionally presents difficulties, especially with regards to deception and the spread of unconfirmed or bogus data. The shut idea of private discussions and gathering talks on WhatsApp makes it provoking for outside substances to screen or reality check the data shared inside these spaces. Deception can spread quickly inside shut gatherings, prompting the intensification of reports, paranoid notions, and wrong news.

The peculiarity of falsehood on WhatsApp acquired huge consideration, particularly with regards to general wellbeing emergencies and races. During the Coronavirus pandemic, for instance, WhatsApp turned into a channel for the quick scattering of both exact general wellbeing data and deluding or bogus cases about the infection, medicines, and preventive measures. The test lies in tracking down a harmony between saving the protection of clients' correspondence and moderating the potential damages related with the spread of falsehood.

WhatsApp has done whatever it takes to address the test of falsehood on its foundation. The presentation of elements like message sending limits, which confine the times a message can be sent, plans to check the fast scattering of unconfirmed data. Furthermore, WhatsApp has teamed up with truth really looking at associations to enable clients to confirm the exactness of sent messages. These actions mirror an acknowledgment of the stage's liability in moderating the adverse consequence of falsehood on open talk.

The crossing point of WhatsApp's part in data dispersal and its impact on political correspondence is critical. The stage plays had a huge impact in political missions and preparation endeavors, particularly in locales where WhatsApp is the essential method of computerized correspondence. Political entertainers influence the stage to interface with citizens, share crusade refreshes, and spread political informing. The immediate and individual nature of correspondence on WhatsApp permits political missions to draw in with citizens in a more cozy way contrasted with conventional media channels.

Be that as it may, the utilization of WhatsApp in political correspondence additionally raises worries about the potential for designated falsehood crusades and the control of general assessment. The confidential idea of messages traded on the stage makes it moving for outer substances to examine or counter bogus stories dispersed inside shut gatherings. Political deception, whether purposefully spread or unintentionally shared, can impact citizen discernments, shape political talk, and effect electing results.

Past individual communications, WhatsApp's job in data spread has suggestions for organizations and associations. The stage's Business Programming interface permits organizations to draw in with clients, give updates, and deal client care through the informing application. This business-to-customer correspondence adds a layer to

WhatsApp's multi-layered job, changing it into a device for corporate data scattering. From request affirmations to item refreshes, organizations influence WhatsApp to disperse opportune and customized data to their client base.

The combination of WhatsApp with business correspondence likewise acquaints contemplations related with information security and assent. Clients should know about how their data is utilized by organizations and ought to can handle the sort and recurrence of messages they get. Finding some kind of harmony between customized correspondence and regarding client security becomes vital for organizations utilizing WhatsApp as a correspondence channel.

The advancing job of WhatsApp in data scattering is intently attached to the more extensive scene of computerized correspondence patterns. As clients progressively go to informing applications for a scope of exercises past private correspondence, including news utilization, shopping, and client service, the limits between various methods of online collaboration obscure. WhatsApp's mix of elements like installments, indexes, and intuitive buttons inside talks mirrors a more extensive pattern in which informing stages try to become thorough centers for different web-based exercises.

The rise of WhatsApp as a stage for monetary exchanges further extends its part in data scattering. The mix of installment functionalities permits clients to send and get cash inside the application, changing WhatsApp into an instrument for monetary data scattering. Clients can get solicitations, installment affirmations, and other monetary updates straightforwardly inside their talk interface. The assembly of informing and monetary exchanges inside a similar stage highlights the liquid idea of data spread in the computerized age.

WhatsApp's job in data dispersal isn't restricted to text based content; the stage's help for mixed media sharing has changed the manner in which clients consume and share visual data. The simplicity with which clients can share pictures, recordings, and voice messages adds to a more extravagant and more powerful type of correspondence. This visual-driven part of data scattering on WhatsApp lines up with more extensive patterns in advanced correspondence, where visual substance frequently overshadows customary text-based correspondence.

The cultural effect of WhatsApp's job in data spread stretches out to social standards, etymological variety, and the conservation of nearby dialects. In districts where WhatsApp is the prevailing informing stage, nearby dialects flourish in computerized spaces. Clients convey in their favored dialects, share content in local vernaculars, and add to the protection of phonetic variety. This social part of data dispersal on WhatsApp mirrors the stage's impact on molding and supporting etymological personalities in the advanced domain.

WhatsApp's effect on data dispersal is entwined with the more extensive cultural ramifications of computerized correspondence stages. The stage adds to the democratization of data, permitting people and networks to take part in a worldwide trade of thoughts. Nonetheless, this democratization accompanies difficulties connected with the uncontrolled spread of deception, the potential for algorithmic polarization, and the effect on customary media biological systems.

The impact of WhatsApp on data spread likewise converges with issues of advanced education and media proficiency. Clients need the abilities to fundamentally assess data, perceive among trustworthy and temperamental sources, and explore the intricacies of online correspondence capably. Computerized proficiency drives assume a critical part in enabling clients to bridle the advantages of WhatsApp's data spread capacities while relieving the dangers related with falsehood.

Looking forward, the future direction of WhatsApp's job in data spread will probably be formed by progressing mechanical headways, client ways of behaving, and administrative turns of events. The stage might keep on advancing its elements, safety efforts, and coordination with other web-based exercises to meet the changing necessities and assumptions for its client base. Moreover, the administrative scene encompassing security, information insurance, and deception will impact how WhatsApp works and the degree to which it can offset data scattering with client assurance.

7.1 Political discourse and activism on WhatsApp

Political talk and activism on WhatsApp have become basic parts of the contemporary advanced scene, reshaping the elements of political correspondence, preparation, and community commitment. WhatsApp, a generally utilized informing stage known for its start to finish encryption and gathering talk capacities, has arisen as a space where people, networks, and political entertainers participate in conversations, share data, and sort out around policy driven issues. This article investigates the complex parts of political talk and activism on WhatsApp, analyzing its effect on equitable support, the difficulties related with the spread of political falsehood, and the developing job of the stage in forming political accounts.

WhatsApp's part in political talk is portrayed by its capacity to work with immediate and quick correspondence among people and gatherings. Political entertainers, going from grassroots activists to ideological groups, influence the stage to interface with constituents, share refreshes, and assemble support.

The stage's start to finish encryption guarantees the protection and security of these political discussions, cultivating a feeling of trust and closeness among members.

The gathering talk highlight on WhatsApp plays had a crucial impact in changing political correspondence. Political missions, backing gatherings, and local area coordinators make gatherings to scatter data, coordinate exercises, and participate progressively conversations with allies. These gatherings act as computerized municipal centers, giving a space to members to offer their viewpoints, clarify some pressing issues, and take part in political discussions. The quickness of correspondence on WhatsApp empowers political entertainers to contact an enormous crowd quickly, encouraging a feeling of local area and fortitude among members.

One of the critical qualities of WhatsApp in political talk lies in its capacity to rise above conventional progressive systems and work with level correspondence.

Dissimilar to one-way correspondence channels, for example, broadcast media, WhatsApp takes into consideration intuitive and decentralized discussions. This even correspondence model engages people to effectively add to political conversations, share assorted viewpoints, and team up on grassroots drives. The stage's job in decentralizing political talk lines up with more extensive patterns of democratizing data and enhancing the voices of underestimated networks.

WhatsApp's effect on political activism stretches out to its part in sorting out and assembling allies for political causes. Activists utilize the stage to facilitate fights, disperse data about occasions, and prepare volunteers. The instantaneousness of correspondence on WhatsApp empowers quick reaction to unfurling occasions, making it a useful asset for on-the-ground sorting out. The stage's ability to interface people across geographic areas adds to the arrangement of virtual networks joined by shared political objectives.

The security elements of WhatsApp, especially its start to finish encryption, add to the trust clients place in the stage for political talk and activism. In conditions where political dispute might confront observation or suppression, the safe and confidential nature of WhatsApp discussions gives a defensive layer to activists and coordinators. The encryption guarantees that the substance of messages stays private, protecting political entertainers from inappropriate examination and oversight.

Notwithstanding, the protection includes that set aside WhatsApp a believed room for political talk likewise present difficulties, especially with regards to political deception and the spread of misleading stories. The start to finish encryption makes it hard for outer elements, including reality checkers and stage overseers, to screen or mediate in confidential gathering discussions. This trademark has prompted worries about the unrestrained scattering of deception inside shut gatherings, where bogus data can spread quickly without outside examination.

The test of political falsehood on WhatsApp acquired huge consideration, especially during races and basic political occasions. The shut idea of private gatherings makes it trying to battle falsehood at scale, as truth checking endeavors are prevented by the stage's protection highlights. Misdirecting content can circle inside protected, closed off areas, supporting existing convictions and impacting political discernments. The convergence of WhatsApp's security design with the potential for the quick spread of deception highlights the fragile harmony between protection privileges and the more extensive cultural ramifications of uncontrolled political lies.

WhatsApp has done whatever it may take to address the test of falsehood on its foundation. The presentation of highlights, for example, message sending limits, which confine the times a message can be sent, means to control the quick spread of unconfirmed data. Furthermore, WhatsApp has teamed up with truth actually taking a look at associations to engage clients to confirm the precision of sent messages. These actions mirror a consciousness of the stage's liability in moderating the adverse consequence of falsehood on political talk.

The transaction between WhatsApp, political talk, and discretionary cycles is a vital part of the stage's impact on just support. Political missions use WhatsApp to interface with electors, share crusade refreshes, and assemble allies. The stage's part in political correspondence turns out to be particularly huge in areas where it is the essential method of computerized association. Be that as it may, the utilization of WhatsApp in political missions likewise brings up issues about the potential for designated political informing, the control of popular assessment, and the requirement for straightforwardness in political correspondence.

The utilization of WhatsApp in political missions raises contemplations connected with the moral utilization of information, elector focusing on, and the potential for algorithmic polarization. Political entertainers can use the individual and conduct information of WhatsApp clients to make designated messages, arriving at explicit segment bunches with custom-made political substance. While designated informing can improve the importance of political correspondence, it additionally raises worries about the expected control of elector opinion and the moral limits of information driven political crusading.

The impact of WhatsApp on political talk stretches out to the connection between traditional press and people in general. Political entertainers utilize the stage to share news refreshes, public statements, and political examinations straightforwardly with their crowd, bypassing customary media watchmen. This direct-to-crowd correspondence model difficulties the conventional job of media delegates in molding general assessment. The dynamic among WhatsApp and established press highlights the developing scene of data dispersal and the manners by which political stories are built and scattered in the computerized age.

WhatsApp's part in political talk crosses with more extensive conversations about the impact of innovation stages on fair cycles. The stage's effect on political stories, general assessment, and municipal commitment brings up issues about the responsibility of advanced stages in the popularity based biological system.

Issues like algorithmic straightforwardness, information protection, and the guideline of political promoting become key to the continuous discussion about the job of innovation in forming political talk.

The reconciliation of WhatsApp into more extensive political correspondence procedures additionally features the requirement for advanced proficiency and media education drives. Clients should foster the abilities to fundamentally assess political data, observe among believable and problematic sources, and explore the intricacies of political correspondence dependably. Computerized education becomes essential for enabling clients to take part in political talk on WhatsApp with an insightful and informed point of view.

The connection between political talk on WhatsApp and more extensive cultural issues, like polarization and social union, is mind boggling and multi-layered. On one hand, WhatsApp's flat correspondence model considers different voices and viewpoints to be heard, adding to a more comprehensive political talk. Then again, the potential for the arrangement of carefully protected areas inside shut bunches raises worries about the support of existing convictions and the fuel of political polarization.

WhatsApp's job in political talk isn't restricted to public or territorial settings; it stretches out to worldwide issues and transnational activism. The stage works with cross-line correspondence and joint effort among people and associations participated in worldwide political developments. Activists use WhatsApp to share data, coordinate activities, and prepare support on a worldwide scale. The stage's capacity to interface people independent of geological limits adds to the development of a globalized computerized open arena.

The advancing job of WhatsApp in political talk additionally crosses with contemplations connected with the guideline of computerized stages. The stage's effect on political correspondence and its suggestions for majority rule processes have provoked conversations about the requirement for administrative systems that balance the conservation of protection with shields against the maltreatment of computerized specialized apparatuses for political control.

Looking forward, the future direction of political talk and activism on WhatsApp will probably be formed by progressing mechanical headways, client ways of behaving, and administrative turns of events. The stage might keep on developing its elements, safety efforts, and protection strategies to address arising difficulties and assumptions. Also, the administrative scene encompassing advanced stages, information protection, and political correspondence will impact how WhatsApp works and the degree to which it can adjust the advantages of political talk with capable stage administration.

All in all, WhatsApp's part in political talk and activism is a diverse and powerful part of the contemporary computerized scene. The stage's capacity to work with direct correspondence, flat associations, and worldwide coordinated effort has changed the elements of political commitment. Be that as it may, challenges connected with deception, protection contemplations, and the effect on fair cycles highlight the complicated interaction among WhatsApp and the more extensive political scene. As innovation and society keep on developing, the job of WhatsApp in political talk will stay a point of convergence in conversations about the crossing point of innovation, a vote based system, and municipal commitment.

7.2 The platform's impact on news consumption and sharing

The effect of web-based entertainment stages on news utilization and sharing has been groundbreaking, and WhatsApp, regardless of being essentially an informing application, assumes a prominent part in forming how data is spread and consumed. This article investigates the multi-layered parts of WhatsApp's effect on news utilization and sharing, analyzing its job in the decentralization of information circulation, the difficulties related with falsehood, and the developing elements of data biological systems inside the stage.

WhatsApp's impact on news utilization is particular in its accentuation on distributed sharing inside shut gatherings. Dissimilar to other web-based entertainment stages with a more open confronting approach, WhatsApp works on the rule of private correspondence, with start to finish encryption guaranteeing the classification of messages. This protection driven plan impacts how news is shared and consumed, making a more close and customized insight for clients.

The stage's gathering visit highlight is a vital driver of its effect on news utilization. Clients can frame bunches in light of shared interests, affiliations, or geographic areas, making miniature networks where news and data are traded. These shut gatherings become center points of data dispersal, permitting clients to share news stories, updates, and media happy with a select crowd. The decentralization of information sharing inside these gatherings adds to a more customized and contextualized way to deal with data utilization.

WhatsApp's job in news utilization meets with more extensive patterns in computerized media, where customers progressively look for customized and significant substance. The stage's gathering driven approach permits clients to organize their news channels inside shut networks, cultivating a feeling of local area and shared interest. This decentralized model difficulties the customary gatekeeping job of media associations, putting more power in the possession of individual clients and gathering directors to shape the stories they consume.

The protection elements of WhatsApp, especially its start to finish encryption, add to the trust clients place in the stage for news sharing. Inside shut gatherings, clients feel a conviction that all is good in sharing and examining news without the apprehension about outer reconnaissance.

This protection driven approach lines up with the developing mindfulness and worries about information security, situating WhatsApp as a space where clients can draw in with news content without the gamble of their collaborations being examined by outer substances.

Notwithstanding, the security includes that set aside WhatsApp a believed room for news sharing likewise present difficulties, especially with regards to deception. The shut idea of private gathering discussions makes it trying for outer substances, including reality checkers and stage executives, to screen or mediate in the spread of deception inside these spaces. Misdirecting content can course inside shut gatherings, where truth checking endeavors are prevented by the stage's security highlights.

The test of deception on WhatsApp acquired conspicuousness, particularly during general wellbeing emergencies and races. Bogus data, tales, and unsubstantiated cases can spread quickly inside shut gatherings, prompting the intensification of deceiving accounts. The decentralized and confidential nature of information utilization on WhatsApp establishes a climate where deception can multiply, affecting clients' discernments and adding to the more extensive test of battling bogus data in the computerized age.

WhatsApp has done whatever it takes to address the test of falsehood on its foundation. The presentation of highlights, for example, message sending limits and the coordinated effort with truth checking associations plan to moderate the fast spread of unconfirmed data. Notwithstanding, the intrinsic strain among protection and the need to control falsehood perseveres, featuring the intricacy of tracking down an equilibrium that jam client security while tending to the negative externalities of unrestrained data scattering.

The effect of WhatsApp on news utilization is additionally apparent in its part in resident reporting and the enhancement of client produced content. Clients can rapidly share observer accounts, photographs, and recordings inside shut gatherings, giving continuous reports on situation as they transpire. This grassroots way to deal with news sharing difficulties conventional media's imposing business model on announcing, empowering people to add to the data biological system and offer points of view that might be ignored by standard outlets.

The quickness and closeness of correspondence on WhatsApp add to the virality of information content inside the stage. Clients frequently depend on direct messages and gathering visits to share making it known, individual perceptions, and investigation with their nearby organization. This shared model of information conveyance, worked with by the stage's elements, mirrors a shift from customary hierarchical models of data spread to a more base up, client driven approach.

The impact of WhatsApp on news utilization reaches out to the connection between established press and its crowd. News associations influence the stage to share refreshes, draw in with perusers, and circulate content straightforwardly to their crowd's cell phones.

The stage turns into an extra dispersion channel for media sources, supplementing their presence on other web-based entertainment stages. The direct-to-crowd correspondence model on WhatsApp challenges conventional media's job as the essential middle person between news makers and shoppers.

The intermingling of information utilization and social cooperation inside WhatsApp adds to the obscuring of limits between data dispersal and relational correspondence. Clients frequently get news refreshes and participate in conversations inside similar stage where they speak with loved ones. This reconciliation of information sharing into the texture of individual correspondence features the developing idea of data utilization in the computerized age, where news isn't recently consumed yet effectively shared and examined inside prompt groups of friends.

The effect of WhatsApp on news utilization is additionally apparent in its part in emergency correspondence and crisis circumstances. During cataclysmic events, public crises, or political turmoil, clients go to WhatsApp to share constant data, look for help, and direction aid ventures. The stage's quickness and universality make it an important instrument for spreading basic updates and interfacing people inside impacted networks. Nonetheless, the decentralized idea of information sharing on

WhatsApp during emergencies likewise raises difficulties connected with the check of data and the potential for the spread of unconfirmed cases.

The convergence of WhatsApp, news utilization, and urban commitment is an essential part of the stage's more extensive cultural effect. The stage turns into a space where clients consume news as well as participate in discussions, discussions, and activism around friendly and policy driven issues. Shut bunches on WhatsApp act as computerized municipal centers, where clients examine recent developments, share viewpoints, and coordinate around causes, adding to a more participatory and democratized way to deal with news utilization.

The developing job of WhatsApp in news utilization additionally converges with contemplations connected with media proficiency and advanced education. As clients become dynamic members in the data biological system, the capacity to basically assess news sources, recognize among sound and questionable data, and explore the intricacies of online news utilization becomes urgent. Media education drives assume a crucial part in enabling clients to draw in with news content on WhatsApp with an insightful and informed point of view.

The future direction of WhatsApp's effect on news utilization will probably be formed by continuous mechanical progressions, client ways of behaving, and administrative turns of events. The stage might keep on developing its highlights, safety efforts, and protection strategies to address arising difficulties and assumptions. Moreover, the administrative scene encompassing computerized stages, falsehood, and news dispersal will impact how WhatsApp works and the degree to which it can adjust the advantages of information utilization with mindful stage administration.

All in all, WhatsApp's effect on news utilization and sharing is described by its accentuation on distributed correspondence, shut collective vibes, and the decentralization of information conveyance. The stage's part in forming how news is consumed reflects more extensive patterns in computerized media, where clients look for additional customized and pertinent substance. Notwithstanding, challenges connected with falsehood, the strain among security and data check, and the developing elements of information utilization inside shut bunches highlight the perplexing transaction among WhatsApp and the more extensive data environment. As innovation and society keep on developing, the job of WhatsApp in news utilization will stay a point of convergence in conversations about the crossing point of innovation, media, and data scattering.

7.3 Societal transformation in information flow and accessibility

The cultural change in data stream and openness has been a sign of the computerized age, reshaping the elements of how data is created, dispersed, and consumed. This paper investigates the diverse parts of cultural change with regards to data stream and availability, inspecting the effect of advanced innovations, the democratization of data, challenges connected with data over-burden and falsehood, and the developing job of people as the two customers and makers of content.

The coming of computerized innovations has changed the manner in which data streams inside social orders. The web, specifically, has filled in as an impetus for the democratization of data, separating customary hindrances to get to and enhancing the voices of people. The democratization of data involves a shift from concentrated, hierarchical models of data scattering to more decentralized, shared communications. Virtual entertainment stages, online discussions, and content-sharing sites have become conductors for a different scope of voices, permitting people to add to and shape the data scene.

Computerized innovations have worked with remarkable admittance to data, engaging people with the capacity to investigate a huge range of viewpoints, news sources, and instructive substance. The democratization of data has destroyed the customary gatekeeping job of media establishments, empowering clients to arrange their data diet and draw in with content that lines up with their inclinations and values. This shift denotes a takeoff from the restricted data wellsprings of the pre-computerized period, growing the skylines of what is open to people.

The democratization of data, in any case, delivers difficulties connected with data over-burden. With a wealth of data accessible at the snap of a button, people are defied with the errand of exploring through a downpour of content to track down dependable and significant data. The sheer volume of data can be overpowering, prompting mental weakness and choice loss of motion. The test lies in getting to data as well as in fostering the abilities to channel, survey, and focus on the huge swath of content accessible.

In addition, the democratization of data has suggestions for the customary power of master voices. While the variety of points of view is a strength, the ascent of client produced content and resident reporting presents the requirement for basic assessment. The test is to perceive trustworthy sources from deception and guarantee that the democratization of data doesn't think twice about quality and precision of the substance consumed.

Deception, energized by the fast spread of unconfirmed or bogus data, is a squeezing worry in the changed data scene. Online entertainment stages, specifically, have been distinguished as courses for the spread of falsehood because of their virality and the carefully protected area impact that enhances specific stories inside shut networks. The test of battling deception includes reality actually looking at endeavors as well as addressing the basic factors that add to the creation and proliferation of bogus accounts.

The cultural change in data stream plays additionally reclassified the part of people as the two shoppers and makers of content. Client produced content, worked with by stages like web-based entertainment, sites, and online discussions, permits people to share their viewpoints, encounters, and innovativeness with a worldwide crowd. The ascent of forces to be reckoned with, content makers, and resident columnists highlights the democratization of content creation, testing conventional orders in media creation.

Be that as it may, this change likewise brings up issues about the credibility and unwavering quality of client created content. The absence of article oversight and the potential for content control present difficulties in guaranteeing the precision and moral principles of data delivered by people. As people explore their jobs as happy makers, basic inquiries arise about the obligation, responsibility, and possible effect of their commitments on the more extensive data environment.

The change in data stream and openness meets with more extensive conversations about the open arena and community commitment. Advanced stages act as spaces where people participate in discussions, offer their viewpoints, and take part in aggregate conversations on cultural issues. The open arena, once bound to customary media and actual spaces, has extended to incorporate advanced spaces where people add to the development of public talk.

The groundbreaking idea of data stream is obvious in political activism and social developments. Computerized innovations, especially web-based entertainment, play had a crucial impact in preparing people, spreading data, and coordinating aggregate activity. Developments like the Middle Easterner Spring, #BlackLivesMatter, and natural activism have utilized advanced stages to enhance their messages, interface with allies, and challenge existing power structures. The capacity to quickly disperse data and coordinate on a worldwide scale has re-imagined the scene of political activism.

The cultural change in data stream and openness is likewise reflected in the domain of schooling. The ascent of internet learning stages, open instructive assets, and computerized libraries has democratized admittance to information. People, regardless of geological area or financial status, can get to instructive substance, take part in web-based courses, and take part in deep rooted learning. This change can possibly span instructive holes, enable students, and reshape customary models of information dispersal.

Notwithstanding, challenges continue guaranteeing evenhanded admittance to instructive assets. The computerized partition, described by differences in admittance to innovation and the web, can fuel existing imbalances. Endeavors to address the computerized partition include growing admittance to innovation as well as considering the financial, social, and etymological variables that impact people's capacity to draw in with advanced instructive substance.

The change in data stream and openness likewise has suggestions for social creation and safeguarding. Computerized stages give spaces to different social articulations, empowering people to share their social legacy, imaginative manifestations, and etymological variety with a worldwide crowd. The conservation of social information and customs is worked with by computerized files, online historical centers, and local area driven drives that influence advanced innovations to defend and share social legacy.

In any case, concerns emerge in regards to the commodification and appointment of social substance in the computerized domain. The simplicity of sharing and duplicating computerized content brings up issues about protected innovation freedoms, social responsiveness, and the dependable utilization of social materials. The cultural change in data stream requires moral contemplations to guarantee that the computerized scene regards and jelly social variety.

The effect of data stream change stretches out to the medical services area. Advanced innovations, telemedicine, and wellbeing data stages have upgraded people's admittance to wellbeing related data and administrations. Patients can get to clinical assets, associate with medical care suppliers from a distance, and participate in wellbeing the executives through computerized stages. This change can possibly enable people with data, work with preventive consideration, and add to more educated medical services navigation.

In any case, challenges connected with the exactness and protection of wellbeing data on computerized stages persevere. The dependable utilization of wellbeing information, the requirement for solid clinical data, and the moral contemplations encompassing the crossing point of innovation and medical care highlight the mind boggling scene of the changed data stream in the wellbeing area.

All in all, the cultural change in data stream and openness is a multi-layered peculiarity that shapes how people access, consume, and produce data. The democratization of data, driven by computerized advances, has destroyed customary progressive systems, engaged people as happy makers, and reclassified the elements of public talk, political activism, schooling, and social articulation. Notwithstanding, difficulties, for example, data over-burden, falsehood, computerized separates, and moral contemplations go with this change, featuring the requirement for an insightful and dependable way to deal with exploring the intricate scene of the computerized data age.

Chapter 8

Future Trends and Societal Implications

The quick development of innovation has been a main thrust in molding the eventual fate of society. As we look forward, a few key patterns arise, each conveying significant ramifications for how we live, work, and connect. These patterns length different spaces, from man-made reasoning to medical services, and their intermingling portrays what's in store.

Man-made reasoning (artificial intelligence) remains at the cutting edge of extraordinary innovations. The coordination of computer based intelligence into different parts of our day to day routines is turning out to be progressively articulated. From menial helpers that get it and answer normal language to AI calculations that power proposal frameworks, artificial intelligence is reshaping the manner in which we connect with data and innovation. In any case, as man-made intelligence frameworks become more complex, inquiries concerning morals, predisposition, and responsibility emerge.

One eminent pattern is the rising independence of artificial intelligence frameworks. We are moving towards a future where machines help as well as pursue choices for our sake. This shift raises worries about the likely loss of human control and the requirement for straightforward dynamic cycles inside computer based intelligence frameworks. Finding some kind of harmony among independence and human oversight will be critical in guaranteeing the mindful turn of events and organization of man-made intelligence advancements.

In equal, the ascent of the Web of Things (IoT) is making a hyperconnected world. Regular items are becoming more intelligent, furnished with sensors and correspondence capacities that empower them to gather and trade information. This availability reaches out past private gadgets to incorporate framework, medical care frameworks, and, surprisingly, whole urban communities. While the commitment of an additional productive and interconnected world is captivating, it likewise raises critical difficulties connected with protection, security, and the potential for maltreatment of individual information.

In addition, progressions in biotechnology are preparing for phenomenal leap forwards in medical services and human improvement. Quality altering innovations, for example, CRISPR, offer the possibility to destroy hereditary illnesses, yet they additionally bring up moral issues about the adjustment of the human germline. Also, the advancement of wearable gadgets and implantable innovations is obscuring the line among man and machine, bringing about the idea of transhumanism. This union of science and innovation challenges conventional thoughts of being human and postures moral difficulties that society should wrestle with.

As we explore these innovative boondocks, the eventual fate of work is going through a significant change. Robotization, filled by man-made intelligence and advanced mechanics, is reshaping enterprises and rethinking the idea of business. While robotization can possibly increment proficiency and let loose human specialists from commonplace undertakings, it additionally raises worries about work relocation and the requirement for reskilling and upskilling to adjust to the developing position market. Finding some kind of harmony between the advantages of computerization and the need to help dislodged laborers will be a basic cultural test.

The eventual fate of instruction is additionally interwoven with these innovative movements. The customary model of training is being tested by internet learning stages, computer generated reality study halls, and customized opportunities for growth fueled by man-made intelligence. The democratization of information is on the ascent, with data turning out to be more open to a worldwide crowd. In any case, guaranteeing equivalent admittance to instructive open doors and tending to the computerized partition are major problems that expect regard for forestall compounding existing cultural disparities.

Ecological supportability is a crosscutting worry that saturates these innovative patterns. The expanded interest for assets to help the developing tech biological system brings up issues about the ecological effect of our mechanical progressions. From the mining of uncommon earth metals for gadgets to the energy utilization of server farms, the natural impression of innovation should be painstakingly thought of. Tracking down reasonable arrangements and taking on eco-accommodating practices will be basic to relieve the biological outcomes of our innovative advancement.

The transaction of these patterns leads to a future where the limits between the physical and computerized universes are progressively obscured. Expanded reality (AR) and computer generated reality (VR) advances are making vivid encounters that upgrade how we see and cooperate with our environmental elements. These advancements have applications past gaming and diversion, stretching out to regions like medical care, training, and distant coordinated effort. Be that as it may, as our computerized and actual real factors combine, inquiries concerning protection, security, and the potential for expanded real factors to shape our impression of the world come to the very front.

In the domain of online protection, what's to come holds the two open doors and difficulties. The rising intricacy and interconnectedness of our advanced frameworks make them more helpless against digital dangers. As society turns out to be more reliant upon computerized framework, the likely effect of digital assaults on basic frameworks, like medical care and energy, turns out to be more serious. Creating hearty network protection measures and encouraging a culture of digital cleanliness will be fundamental for defend against these arising dangers.

The international scene is additionally going through huge changes in light of these mechanical patterns. The race for innovative strength is molding worldwide relations and energizing rivalry among countries. Issues, for example, information power, protected innovation privileges, and the guideline of arising advances are becoming central focuses in strategic conversations. Finding some kind of harmony between encouraging advancement and tending to worldwide difficulties cooperatively will be urgent in exploring the intricacies of the mechanically determined international scene.

In the midst of these groundbreaking patterns, the job of morals in innovation turns out to be progressively fundamental. As we push the limits of what is conceivable, moral contemplations should direct the turn of events and organization of new advances. Guaranteeing straightforwardness, responsibility, and inclusivity in the dynamic cycles encompassing innovation is crucial for assemble trust and moderate likely damages. The moral structure ought to reach out past the makers of innovation to incorporate policymakers, organizations, and society at large.

All in all, what's to come holds an embroidery of mechanical progressions that will reshape the structure holding the system together. From the rising independence of computer based intelligence frameworks to the hyperconnectivity empowered by the Web of Things, the union of biotechnology and advanced innovations to the change of work and schooling, these patterns are interconnected and present the two potential open doors and difficulties. Exploring this complicated scene requires an all encompassing and moral methodology that thinks about the cultural ramifications of our innovative decisions. As we stand at the edge of this innovative boondocks, the choices we make today will shape the universe of tomorrow. It is occupant upon us to explore these progressions mindfully, with a sharp consciousness of the expected effect on people, networks, and the planet in general.

8.1 Speculations on the future role of WhatsApp

As we peer into the fate of correspondence innovation, WhatsApp remains at the front as a stage that has not just changed the manner in which we interface with each other yet in addition holds the possibility to shape the future scene of computerized correspondence. From its modest starting points as a straightforward informing application to its ongoing status as a multi-layered stage offering voice and video calls, bunch talks, and mixed media sharing, WhatsApp has turned into a necessary piece of our day to day routines. Hypothesizing on its future job includes thinking about innovative progressions as well as cultural movements and the advancing assumptions for clients.

One possible direction for WhatsApp is its proceeded with combination with other Facebook-possessed stages, making a more consistent and interconnected insight for clients. The blend of WhatsApp with Instagram and Facebook Courier has proactively started, permitting clients to easily impart across these stages. This mix could develop further, offering a brought together informing experience that rises above individual applications. While this could upgrade client comfort, it likewise raises worries about information security and the centralization of correspondence power inside a solitary corporate substance.

The development of WhatsApp as a correspondence center reaches out past message based messages. The stage's joining of voice and video calling highlights has previously situated it as an extensive specialized device. Looking forward, progressions in expanded reality (AR) and computer generated reality (VR) might actually reshape the manner in which we cooperate on WhatsApp. Envision a future where clients can take part in virtual gatherings, share vivid encounters, or even go to occasions inside the WhatsApp stage. This speculative reconciliation of AR and VR innovations could reclassify the idea of online correspondence, offering a more similar and drawing in experience.

In addition, the job of man-made reasoning (artificial intelligence) in forming the eventual fate of WhatsApp couldn't possibly be more significant. Artificial intelligence fueled chatbots and robotized informing frameworks are now being investigated, permitting organizations to give moment client care and empowering clients to productively get to data more. The future might see a development of these abilities, with computer based intelligence turning out to be more incorporated into ordinary discussions on WhatsApp. This could go from customized content ideas to keen robotized reactions, making associations on the stage more powerful and custom-made to individual inclinations.

As WhatsApp keeps on advancing, its effect on business correspondence is probably going to increase. The stage has previously presented business records and highlights like index sharing for little undertakings. Looking forward, we can expect a more vigorous environment for business correspondence inside WhatsApp.

This could incorporate high level client relationship the board (CRM) instruments, coordinated installment frameworks, and modern examination to assist businesses with better comprehension and draw in with their clients. The obscuring of lines among individual and business correspondence on WhatsApp could reclassify the manner in which organizations associate with their crowd.

One charming road for hypothesis is the possible combination of WhatsApp with arising advancements like blockchain. The joining of blockchain could upgrade security and protection highlights on the stage, guaranteeing start to finish encryption and giving clients more prominent command over their information. Furthermore, blockchain-based arrangements could work with secure and straightforward exchanges inside the stage, opening up opportunities for cryptographic money joining. This speculative combination of WhatsApp with blockchain innovation could address a portion of the protection worries that have been related with unified informing stages.

The worldwide idea of WhatsApp delivers contemplations of social and provincial transformations. The stage has proactively presented highlights like language-explicit stickers and regionalized content proposals. Looking forward, WhatsApp could additionally tailor its contributions to take special care of the different phonetic and social inclinations of its client base. This could include the combination of continuous interpretation highlights, permitting clients to convey consistently across language boundaries. The restriction of content and administrations could make WhatsApp significantly more open and interesting to a worldwide crowd.

A charming viewpoint to consider is the potential for WhatsApp to assume a part in molding political talk and community commitment. The stage has proactively been used for political correspondence and activism in different areas of the planet. Hypothesizing on the future, WhatsApp could turn into a more conspicuous player in working with community discourse, citizen commitment, and, surprisingly, the spread of dependable data during decisions. This, nonetheless, raises worries about the spread of falsehood and the requirement for vigorous instruments to check and validate data shared on the stage.

The availability and universality of cell phones have been key drivers in the broad reception of WhatsApp. Looking forward, the development of specialized gadgets could impact the stage's future job. The ascent of wearable innovation, increased reality glasses, and other imaginative gadgets might open up new roads for how clients associate with WhatsApp. Envision a future where clients can send messages or settle on decisions straightforwardly from their savvy glasses, or where WhatsApp flawlessly coordinates with the up and coming age of specialized gadgets. This speculative advancement could rethink the client experience and further incorporate WhatsApp into the texture of our day to day routines.

The developing idea of security concerns is one more aspect to consider while hypothesizing about WhatsApp's future job. As conversations around information security strengthen, clients are turning out to be more aware of how their data is dealt with by computerized stages. WhatsApp's obligation to start to finish encryption has been a foundation of its protection highlights. Nonetheless, the future might see a much more noteworthy accentuation on client control and straightforwardness. Hypothetically, clients could oversee the information they share, with choices to set explicit security inclinations for various kinds of collaborations.

Taking into account the quick headways in biometric innovation, one more speculative road is the combination of biometric validation highlights on WhatsApp. This could include utilizing facial acknowledgment or unique finger impression checking to upgrade the security of the stage and smooth out client confirmation. While this could give an extra layer of safety, it additionally raises worries about the likely abuse of biometric information and the requirement for powerful shields to safeguard client security.

The cultural ramifications of WhatsApp's future job stretch out past the domain of innovation. The stage has proactively assumed a huge part in associating individuals, cultivating connections, and crossing over correspondence holes. Looking forward, the advancing idea of computerized correspondence brings up issues about the effect on relational connections and social elements. Hypothetically, the rising dependence on informing applications for correspondence could impact the manner in which we structure and keep up with connections, with suggestions for the quality and profundity of our associations.

One must likewise consider the expected job of WhatsApp in tending to squeezing worldwide difficulties. The stage's inescapable reach and quick correspondence abilities could be utilized for social great. Theoretically, WhatsApp could turn into a critical device in dispersing constant data during crises, working with local area driven drives, or preparing support for social and natural causes. Be that as it may, this additionally brings up moral issues about the obligation of stages like WhatsApp in forming public talk and affecting cultural qualities.

All in all, estimating on the future job of WhatsApp includes imagining a scene where mechanical headways, cultural movements, and client assumptions combine. From consistent reconciliation with different stages to the joining of expanded reality and man-made brainpower, the conceivable outcomes are huge. The stage's job in business correspondence, its likely combination with blockchain, and its effect on worldwide political talk add layers to the speculative story. As we explore this unsure landscape, it is fundamental to think about the innovative elements as well as the moral and cultural ramifications of WhatsApp's future development. decisions in the turn of events and organization of these advances will shape the manner in which we convey, associate, and connect with each other in the years to come.

8.2 The platform's potential influence on upcoming cultural shifts

Looking at the direction of contemporary stages, for example, web-based entertainment and specialized instruments, divulges a significant effect on social elements. Among these stages, WhatsApp arises as a critical player, in working with correspondence as well as in possibly forming forthcoming social movements. As social orders internationally become more interconnected, the impact of advanced stages on social standards, values, and ways of behaving turns out to be progressively articulated. Hypothesizing on the likely impact of WhatsApp on forthcoming social movements includes diving into different viewpoints, from correspondence examples to the spread of data and the development of social communications.

One aspect to consider is the advancing idea of correspondence worked with by WhatsApp. The stage's pervasiveness has previously changed how people and networks convey. From texting to voice and video calls, WhatsApp has turned into a vital piece of the advanced correspondence scene. Looking forward, the stage's impact on correspondence examples might reach out to the obscuring of conventional limits among individual and expert associations. The simplicity of correspondence presented by WhatsApp might prompt a more liquid trade of thoughts, cultivating a social shift where people flawlessly explore among individual and business related conversations inside a similar stage.

In addition, the ascent of gathering visits on WhatsApp has suggestions for the elements of groups of friends. The stage's gathering highlights work with continuous discussions among different people, rising above geological hindrances. Hypothetically, this could add to the arrangement of globalized social networks, where people from various areas of the planet participate in shared interests, conversations, and joint efforts. The potential social shift includes a more interconnected and different social scene, separating conventional storehouses and encouraging a feeling of worldwide local area.

As the stage keeps on advancing, its part in molding social accounts turns out to be progressively huge. WhatsApp has previously been used as an instrument for political activism, social trade, and the dispersal of data. Estimating on the future, the stage could assume a more unmistakable part in forming public talk and impacting social stories. This could include the intensification of different voices, the democratization of data, and the assistance of grassroots developments that challenge existing social standards. Be that as it may, it likewise raises worries about the spread of deception and the requirement for instruments to guarantee the precision and unwavering quality of data shared on the stage.

The sight and sound sharing abilities of WhatsApp add to its possible impact on social movements. The stage's part in the fast dispersal of pictures, recordings, and other sight and sound substance has suggestions for how social patterns and peculiarities spread.

Hypothetically, WhatsApp could turn into an impetus for the virality of social articulations, from images to imaginative manifestations. This might add to the fast reception and transformation of social patterns, making a more interconnected and dynamic social scene.

Moreover, the combination of increased reality (AR) and augmented reality (VR) advances into WhatsApp could reclassify how social encounters are shared. Envision a future where clients can take part in virtual comprehensive developments, share vivid encounters, or investigate social legacy through AR-upgraded highlights. This speculative coordination of innovation into social articulation could obscure the lines between the advanced and actual domains, offering new roads for inventive articulation and social investigation.

The stage's effect on language and phonetic variety is one more feature to consider. WhatsApp's language-explicit elements, like multilingual stickers and regionalized content proposals, as of now mirror an attention to etymological variety. Hypothetically, the stage could develop to additional help and safeguard minority dialects, adding to a more comprehensive portrayal of etymological variety in computerized spaces. This could, thus, impact social articulations and stories, cultivating a social shift towards more noteworthy appreciation for semantic pluralism.

Looking at the job of WhatsApp in molding social movements requires thinking about its effect on conventional types of media and data utilization. The stage's job in scattering news and data has been both adulated for its quickness and censured for spreading misinformation potential. As the stage advances, there is hypothesis about its part in rethinking the elements of information utilization and data sharing. This might include a shift towards more customized and intelligent news encounters, where clients draw in with and add to the formation of information content inside the stage.

The possible joining of blockchain innovation into WhatsApp adds one more layer to the hypothesis. Blockchain's highlights, like straightforwardness and decentralization, could address worries about the veracity of data on the stage. Hypothetically, blockchain could be utilized to confirm the legitimacy of information sources, forestall the spread of phony news, and guarantee a more reliable data environment inside WhatsApp. This could add to a social shift towards more prominent confidence in computerized stages as wellsprings of dependable data.

Moreover, WhatsApp's part in the advancement of online networks merits investigating. The stage's gathering highlights currently empower the development of specialty networks in view of shared interests, convictions, or affiliations. Hypothetically, this could prompt a social shift where people progressively search out and draw in with networks that line up with their qualities, adding to the development of computerized subcultures. These subcultures might impact more extensive social stories, testing standard points of view and encouraging a more different social scene.

The impact of WhatsApp on social movements reaches out to the domain of monetary communications. The stage's joining of business highlights, for example, business records and inventory sharing, has suggestions for how trade is led. Hypothetically, WhatsApp could turn into a focal center for internet business, where organizations draw in with clients, grandstand items, and work with exchanges inside the stage. This shift could reclassify the elements of internet shopping and add to a social change towards additional incorporated and customized business communications.

As WhatsApp keeps on assuming a focal part in molding social elements, the topic of its effect on individual prosperity emerges. The stage's impact on psychological wellness, social connections, and self-insight is an area of concern and hypothesis. The steady availability worked with by WhatsApp might add to an "consistently on" culture, obscuring the limits among work and individual life. Hypothetically, this could prompt a social shift where people focus on computerized prosperity, defining limits on their internet based connections and looking for a better harmony between the virtual and the physical.

Additionally, the possible combination of biometric confirmation highlights into WhatsApp brings up issues about protection and security. While biometric verification could improve the security of the stage, it likewise presents worries about the assortment and capacity of touchy individual information. Hypothetically, clients might turn out to be more aware of their advanced impression and request more prominent command over how their biometric data is utilized inside the stage. This social shift towards elevated security mindfulness could impact more extensive conversations about computerized morals and client freedoms.

The cultural ramifications of WhatsApp's likely impact on forthcoming social movements stretch out to contemplations of inclusivity and portrayal. The stage's effect on social stories and articulations might add to a more comprehensive portrayal of different voices and points of view. Theoretically, WhatsApp could turn into a space where underrepresented networks track down a stage for self-articulation, testing existing social standards and encouraging a more fair social scene.

All in all, guessing on WhatsApp's likely impact on impending social movements includes imagining a future where correspondence designs, data spread, and social connections are profoundly entwined with the highlights and elements of the stage. From the development of online networks to the combination of arising advancements, the conceivable outcomes are immense. As WhatsApp keeps on forming the manner in which we interface, impart, and share, its impact on social elements will probably heighten. Exploring this developing scene requires a nuanced comprehension of the transaction among innovation and culture, with a sharp consciousness of the expected cultural ramifications of WhatsApp's job in forming social movements.

8.3 Concluding thoughts on the lasting impact of WhatsApp on global communication culture.

Pondering the direction and development of WhatsApp, it becomes clear that the stage has made a permanent imprint on worldwide correspondence culture. As we draw finishing up contemplations on its enduring effect, it is fundamental to consider the complex aspects through which WhatsApp has impacted the manner in which people and networks associate, share data, and shape social stories.

As a matter of some importance, WhatsApp's job as a specialized device has changed the scene of relational communications. The stage's initiation as a straightforward informing application denoted a takeoff from customary SMS informing, offering a more practical and include rich other option. The presentation of voice and video calling additionally extended its capacities, furnishing clients with a flexible stage for constant correspondence. The enduring effect lies in how WhatsApp has become imbued in the texture of day to day existence, filling in as a conductor for both individual and expert discussions.

The gathering visit include has been a foundation of WhatsApp's prosperity, cultivating a feeling of local area and network. Whether utilized for family conversations, cooperative work attempts, or associating with companions, bunch visits have become fundamental to current correspondence elements. The stage's capacity to work with moment correspondence among numerous people, paying little heed to geological distances, has reclassified the thought of groups of friends. This enduring effect has added to a more interconnected reality where connections are supported and sustained through computerized channels.

The interactive media sharing capacities of WhatsApp have sped up the speed at which data, patterns, and social articulations circle universally. The stage's part in spreading pictures, recordings, and images has added to the fast reception of social peculiarities. From viral difficulties to shared social references, WhatsApp plays had a significant impact in molding the climate of the computerized period. This enduring effect reaches out past simple correspondence to impact how social patterns arise, develop, and resound across different networks.

Besides, the impact of WhatsApp on language and etymological variety is an imperative part of its effect. The stage's help for multilingual correspondence, language-explicit elements, and regionalized content suggestions mirrors an affirmation of the different etymological scene of its client base. This enduring effect adds to a computerized climate where semantic pluralism is esteemed, and clients can put themselves out there in their favored dialects, cultivating a more comprehensive and socially rich correspondence experience.

The coordination of business highlights into WhatsApp has reclassified the scene of computerized trade and client commitment. The stage's part in working with business accounts, list sharing, and client correspondence has situated it as a urgent device for business visionaries and private companies. This enduring effect reaches out to the democratization of business correspondence, permitting endeavors, everything being equal, to straightforwardly draw in with their crowd. WhatsApp's impact on monetary communications has added to a social shift where computerized stages assume a focal part in business exercises.

WhatsApp's expected intermingling with arising advancements like increased reality (AR) and augmented reality (VR) opens new roads for social encounters. The speculative joining of AR and VR innovations into the stage could reclassify how clients draw in with social substance, from virtual occasions to vivid narrating. This enduring effect might add to a social scene where computerized stages act as specialized instruments as well as vivid entryways for social investigation and articulation.

The stage's impact on political talk and city commitment is a two sided deal, stamping both positive and concerning viewpoints. WhatsApp has been a course for political correspondence, activism, and the spread of data during races and social developments. This enduring effect highlights the stage's job in forming public talk and activating networks. In any case, the spread of deception and the potential for closed quarters present difficulties that need cautious thought. WhatsApp's effect on political and social stories underscores the requirement for capable stage administration and client mindfulness.

As WhatsApp explores the advancing scene of online networks, its enduring effect on the development of computerized subcultures is obvious. The stage's gathering highlights empower people with shared interests or affiliations to associate, making specialty networks inside the advanced domain. This enduring effect adds to a social scene where online subcultures assume a critical part in forming social articulations and testing standard viewpoints.

Security and security contemplations have been integral to WhatsApp's ethos, with the execution of start to finish encryption and a guarantee to client information insurance. This enduring effect has situated WhatsApp as a stage that focuses on client protection, ingraining a feeling of trust among its client base. Be that as it may, the developing scene of computerized protection and information security requires nonstop carefulness and transformation to arising difficulties.

The likely mix of biometric confirmation highlights into WhatsApp features the stage's obligation to improving security while presenting contemplations about client information. This enduring effect highlights the sensitive harmony between safety efforts and client protection, underlining the requirement for straightforward correspondence and strong shields.

As biometric innovation turns out to be more predominant, its execution inside WhatsApp reflects more extensive cultural conversations about the convergence of innovation and individual privileges.

The worldwide reach and openness of WhatsApp add to its enduring effect on crossing over social holes and cultivating a feeling of worldwide local area. The stage's capacity to interface people from different foundations, work with multifaceted correspondence, and extension geological distances has added to a more interconnected world. This enduring effect stretches out past private associations to impact how social comprehension and appreciation are encouraged in the computerized age.

In taking into account WhatsApp's enduring effect on worldwide correspondence culture, it is basic to recognize the difficulties that go with its far reaching reception. The stage's impact on data dispersal has raised worries about the spread of deception, advanced closed quarters, and the likely disintegration of decisive reasoning. This enduring effect highlights the obligation of advanced stages to address these difficulties through vigorous substance control, truth really looking at systems, and client instruction.

All in all, WhatsApp's excursion from a basic informing application to a diverse correspondence stage has left a getting through engrave on worldwide correspondence culture. Its enduring effect is apparent in the change of relational associations, the speed increase of social patterns, the redefinition of semantic variety, and the democratization of business correspondence. As WhatsApp proceeds to develop and shape the manner in which people and networks interface, it fills in as an impression of the more extensive social changes in the computerized age. Exploring its effect requires an insightful harmony between mechanical development, client strengthening, and cultural obligation to guarantee that the getting through tradition of WhatsApp is one that improves worldwide correspondence culture.

Chapter 9

Conclusion

In the consistently developing scene of computerized correspondence, WhatsApp has arisen as a prevailing player, molding the manner in which individuals associate and offer data universally. Past its essential job as an informing stage, WhatsApp plays had a crucial impact in impacting social elements, prompting a remarkable social shift. This shift envelops changes in correspondence designs, social collaborations, and how data is spread.

One of the key components adding to WhatsApp's social effect is its universal presence. With north of two billion month to month dynamic clients starting around my last information update in January 2022, WhatsApp has turned into an essential piece of day to day existence for people across different socioeconomics. Its straightforwardness, cross-stage usefulness, and start to finish encryption have settled on it a favored decision for correspondence, encouraging a degree of closeness and promptness that rises above geological limits.

The idea of correspondence on WhatsApp has gone through a change, testing customary methods of connection. The stage's texting highlights have diminished the idleness in correspondence, permitting clients to participate progressively discussions paying little mind to actual distances. This shift has sped up the speed of correspondence, establishing a climate where ideal reactions are normal as well as essential to the smoothness of discussions.

Besides, the presentation of media sharing abilities on WhatsApp has reclassified the manner in which individuals articulate their thoughts. The trading of pictures, recordings, and voice messages has added a layer of lavishness to discussions, empowering clients to convey feelings and subtleties that message alone could neglect to catch. This sight and sound driven approach has added to the stage's allure across ages, making it a flexible device for individual and expert correspondence.

The peculiarity of gathering talks on WhatsApp has likewise assumed a huge part in reshaping social elements. Bunch visits, whether among companions, family, or associates, have become virtual spaces for aggregate independent direction, coordination, and the sharing of encounters. These computerized networks frequently reflect true groups of friends, affecting how people see and draw in with their informal organizations.

In any case, the accommodation of gathering visits accompanies its own arrangement of difficulties. The steady stream of messages, warnings, and the covering discussions inside a gathering can prompt data over-burden and a feeling of computerized weakness. This has incited conversations about the requirement for computerized decorum and the harmony between remaining associated and dealing with the possible drawbacks of consistent network.

Past private correspondence, WhatsApp has turned into a noticeable stage for the dispersal of data, both formal and casual. The sending highlight, while expected to work with the sharing of important substance, has been a blade that cuts both ways. The straightforwardness with which data can be sent to different contacts has prompted the fast spread of information, tales, and falsehood. WhatsApp has wrestled with this issue, executing measures, for example, message sending cutoff points to control the unrestrained scattering of unconfirmed data.

The effect of WhatsApp on friendly impact is especially apparent in its job during huge occasions, like races or public developments. The stage has been a course for political talk, activism, and the preparation of networks. Its capacity to work with the fast spread of data has brought up issues about the moral utilization of informing stages in impacting general assessment and molding aggregate stories.

The approach of WhatsApp Business has additionally extended the stage's venture into the domain of trade and client commitment. Little and medium-sized ventures (SMEs) influence WhatsApp as an instrument for client correspondence, request handling, and showcasing. This combination of business and correspondence on a solitary stage has suggestions for the manner in which people see and connect with brands, obscuring the lines among individual and business correspondence.

The social effect of WhatsApp isn't bound to its specialized highlights however reaches out to the standards and ways of behaving that have arisen inside the stage's environment. The utilization of emoticons, GIFs, and stickers has turned into its very own language, empowering clients to communicate feelings and convey setting in a brief and outwardly captivating way. This shift towards a more visual and emotive type of correspondence has impacted the manner in which people create their computerized personas.

The thought of "status" on WhatsApp, where clients can share refreshes as text, photographs, or recordings, has made a space for self-articulation. This element, suggestive of online entertainment courses of events, permits people to feature their contemplations, encounters, and mind-sets to their contacts. The organized idea of notices mirrors a craving for self-show, adding to the development of online characters inside the WhatsApp people group.

Similarly as with any social shift, the effect of WhatsApp on friendly impact isn't uniform across all socioeconomics. Factors like age, geographic area, and social setting assume a huge part in forming how people see and utilize the stage. While more youthful ages might embrace the visual and intelligent parts of WhatsApp, more seasoned ages could esteem the stage for its effortlessness and productivity in correspondence.

The impact of WhatsApp on accepted practices and decorums is additionally obvious in the obscuring of limits among individual and expert correspondence. The stage's usability and openness have prompted the joining of business related conversations inside private talks, testing conventional qualifications among expert and individual spaces. This pattern has suggestions for balance between serious and fun activities and the developing idea of expert connections in a computerized age.

Protection concerns have been a relentless topic in conversations encompassing WhatsApp's social effect. While start to finish encryption gives a layer of safety, the stage has confronted examination for its information imparting strategies to its parent organization, Facebook. This pressure among protection and availability highlights the more extensive cultural discussion about the compromises inborn in the computerized time, where the accommodation of interconnectedness comes at the expense of individual information openness.

The impact of WhatsApp on friendly elements likewise reaches out to the domain of emotional wellness. The steady network worked with by informing stages can add to sensations of social examination, FOMO (feeling of dread toward passing up a major opportunity), and the strain to organize a positive web-based presence. Moreover, the promptness of correspondence on WhatsApp can obscure the limits between private space and computerized cooperations, raising worries about the effect of consistent availability on mental prosperity.

The developing idea of WhatsApp's social effect prompts reflection on the obligation of tech organizations in molding cultural standards. As a stage with worldwide reach, WhatsApp can possibly impact individual ways of behaving as well as more extensive social patterns. The test lies in offsetting advancement with moral contemplations, guaranteeing that the social shift worked with by informing stages lines up with upsides of inclusivity, protection, and dependable innovation use.

All in all, WhatsApp's social shift is a multi-layered peculiarity that envelops changes in correspondence designs, social communications, and the spread of data. The stage's universality, texting highlights, sight and sound capacities, and gathering talks have re-classified how people interface and draw in with each other. The impact of WhatsApp stretches out past private correspondence to remember its job for molding accepted practices, affecting popular assessment, and influencing psychological wellness.

As WhatsApp keeps on developing, its social effect will probably go through additional changes, affected by mechanical progressions, client ways of behaving, and cultural assumptions. Exploring the intricacies of this social shift requires a nuanced comprehension of the interconnected idea of computerized correspondence and its suggestions for the manner in which we connect with each other in an undeniably associated world.